100 WALKS IN
West Sussex

compiled by

DEN SKINNER

The Crowood Press

First published in 1995 by
The Crowood Press Ltd
Ramsbury
Marlborough
Wiltshire SN8 2HR

This impression 1998

British Library Cataloguing-in-Publication Data
A catalogue record for this book is
available from the British Library

ISBN 1 85223 847 X

All maps by Janet Powell

Typeset by Carreg Limited, Ross-on-Wye, Herefordshire

Printed by Redwood Books, Trowbridge, Wiltshire

CONTENTS

Publisher's Note

We very much hope that you enjoy the routes presented in this book, which has been compiled with the aim of allowing you to explore the area in the best possible way – on foot.

We strongly recommend that you take the relevant map for the area, and for this reason we list the appropriate Ordnance Survey maps for each route. Whilst the details and descriptions given for each walk were accurate at time of writing, the countryside is constantly changing, and a map will be essential if, for any reason, you are unable to follow the given route. It is good practice to carry a map and use it so that you are always aware of your exact location.

We cannot be held responsible if some of the details in the route descriptions are found to be inaccurate, but should be grateful if walkers would advise us of any major alterations. Please note that whenever you are walking in the countryside you are on somebody else's land, and we must stress that you should *always* keep to established rights of way, and *never* cross fences, hedges or other boundaries unless there is a clear crossing point.

Remember the country code:

Enjoy the country and respect its life and work
Guard against all risk of fire
Fasten all gates
Keep dogs under close control
Keep to public footpaths across all farmland
Use gates and stiles to cross field boundaries
Leave all livestock, machinery and crops alone
Take your litter home
Help to keep all water clean
Protect wildlife, plants and trees
Make no unnecessary noise

The walks are listed by length – from approximately 1 to 12 miles – but the amount of time taken will depend on the fitness of the walkers and the time spent exploring any points of interest along the way. Nearly all the walks are circular and most offer recommendations for refreshments.

Good walking.

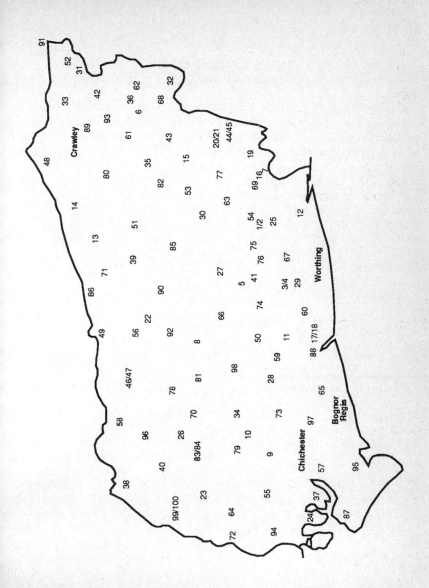

Maps: OS Sheets Landranger 198; Pathfinder 1287.
Two short walks in this old market town.
Start: At 178112, Fletcher's Croft car park.

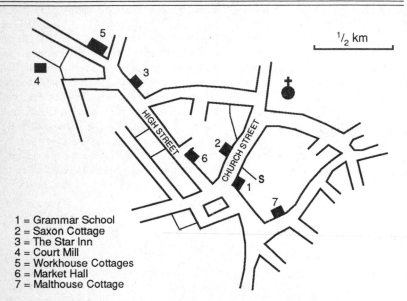

1 = Grammar School
2 = Saxon Cottage
3 = The Star Inn
4 = Court Mill
5 = Workhouse Cottages
6 = Market Hall
7 = Malthouse Cottage

Turn right on the footpath that runs in front of the Steyning Centre. School Lane takes you between buildings of the grammar school: opposite on Church Street stands one of Steyning's remaining pubs, the Norfolk Arms. Turn right and beside the much photographed Saxon Cottage, with its 'cat slide' thatched roof, veer left into Chantry Green. The three cottages were originally a single, timber-framed house. Next door, the Queen Anne Chantry House was once home to the poet, W B Yeats. Continue to Smuggler's Cottage, where a light was placed in a dormer window when excise men were active. Turn left into a narrow path, and left again to a road. Cross to another car park and look back to the clock tower above No 72, the Old Market Hall. This building has served as town hall, police and fire stations. Walk down the road: No 69 was a forge, No 75 was, in the 18th century, the Duke of Norfolk's shooting box. Sussex oxen were once shod at Chanctonbury Cottage. Just prior to the Star, the original mill stream is culverted beneath the road. Opposite is Sir Georges Place. Go along this to a footpath leaving, right, beside Court Mill. Cross a diverted stream, then fork right for Mouse Lane. Before the main road there are three cottages converted from one Wealden timber-framed building: the name 'Workhouse Cottages' confirms their previous usage. Re-trace the High Street to a twitten adjacent to No 97. This leads to Charton Street: No 23, the Soldiers Return was once an ale house. Return through the car park and turn right. The building housing Lloyds has been a bank since 1847, the emblem of the first bank, a carved wheatsheaf faces you across the street. Go right beside the second coaching inn, the White Horse, into Sheep Pen Lane. In the wall opposite the gateway to Newhams is a plaque recording the old names for this lane. Go left on a grassy path. As you collect Dog Leg Lane look left: there is an old mounting block built into the wall. The flint wall on the left, with a brick string course, contains odd pieces of stone, believed to have been removed from the church in the 16th century. The dry watercourse at the foot of the wall was the Singwell Stream: Springwells, the house on the corner of the High Street, is a corruption of this name. Turn left, pass the old pump and cattle trough, then follow the causeway past Penfold House, cross into Church Street. Go past the old grammar school: the Tuck Shop was housed in cottage No 4. On arriving at School Lane either return to the start or continue ahead for another a longer walk.

Look at the buildings on the other side of the road: the plaque over No 23 confirmed the residence of the MP for neighbouring Bramber. At the time the parish boundaries were in dispute. Fork left into Church Lane and enter the churchyard by the entrance adjacent to Gatewick. The old port of Portus Cuthmanii was sited to the north and east of the church. Note the two sanctuary rings on the 14th-century church door: by grasping these a fugitive could obtain temporary protection from the law. Back on the road, go left, then fork right into Cripps Lane. Pass a new close and turn right into Jervis Lane. The interesting buildings are at the further end. Opposite Castle Lane Malthouse Cottage was once a brewery. Next door was the officers' quarters when troops were stationed here in readiness for the threatened Napoleonic invasion. Around the corner in the High Street is the unmistakable outline of another old inn – the Three Tuns. Again the name remains in the new development. Now continue on familiar ground back to Church Street.

REFRESHMENTS:
Numerous!

Walks 3 & 4   **THE LONG FURLONG**   4m (6¹/₂km)
or 6m (9¹/₂km)

Maps: OS Sheets Landranger 197 and 198; Pathfinder 1306.
*A walk with an optional extension around an unusual downland
feature.*
Start: At 096066, Clapham Church.

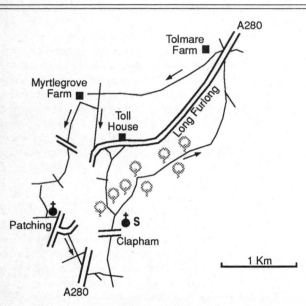

Clapham church is set against woodland and reached by an unmade track from the
village street.

    Leave the churchyard over a stile in the north-east corner and cross a field. Go
half-left into trees. The route now follows a track that alternates between woods and
fields. The traffic noise from below confirms when you have reached the crest of the
hill: continue into the open and follow a fence. On joining a bridleway, turn left, then
left again at the road used as a public path (RUPP) which soon slopes down to the
A280 at the head of the valley. Cross, with care, and almost immediately double back
left on a track to the south of Tolmare Farm. The track dips then climbs over the low
shoulder of Blackpatch Hill. At a gate which marks the parish boundary, the track

ends. The fence running to the left falls to a road where the old toll house tries to hide between trees. Continue through fields to join the access drive from Myrtle Grove. Turn left. After 200 yards, the longer route turns right.

The shorter route goes down to meet the **Long Furlong** road at a sharp bend. Cross, with care, to a stile and climb a path. At a fence and path junction, go over a stile and walk beside a fence. Now slope up to a wood. You may notice that this wood, in common with the other above Clapham, consists largely of hazel, a species of tree not usually associated with the Downs. Keep to the main track for a short stroll back to the church.

The longer route follows the power poles to a fence and gate. Bear left with the path towards Patching Hill. Turn left for a few yards to stables, then right into an overgrown area. On reaching open downland, veer half-left to an obvious track climbing between the reservoirs. Cross the route of the Angmering Park walks(seeWalks 17 and 18), then fork towards the church. Zig-zag through Patching, going left at the farm, right along The Street and left again at the T-junction. Leave the road on the bend, dropping right through fields. Skirt a pond and go to the right of a cricket pitch. Cross the main road, with care, into the entrance of the county works yard. Keep outside the mesh fence, then turn left on a track that is followed through the village back to the church.

POINTS OF INTEREST:

Clapham Church – The church contains many monuments to the Shelley family who lived at Michelgrove for over 350 years. One brass shows a 16th-century Shelley with his wife and fourteen children (seven pigeon pairs). The low window in the chancel could have been a squint allowing unfortunates a view to services.

Long Furlong – This downland feature, bordered on the north by the A280, is a sombre and gloomy place in winter for the sun struggles to rise over the skyline. The road was built in 1818 as a coaching route from Clapham to Findon. The castellated toll house has an arched recess designed to hold the toll board with its list of current charges.

REFRESHMENTS:

None on the route, but numerous possibilities in nearby Worthing.

Walk 5   STORRINGTON AND SULLINGTON   4¹/₂m (7km)

Maps: OS Sheets Landranger 197 and 198; Pathfinder 1287.

Visiting two under-down settlements – one large modern and bland, the other small ancient and interesting.

Start: At 087119, Chantry Post car park.

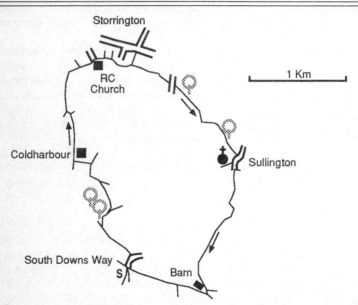

Leave the car park and retreat down the single track road for 150 yards to reach a path across the top of Chantry Hill. Below, the houses at Storrington appear snow flecked with their white embellishments reflecting any available sunlight. Fork right around the head of the coombe, then walk below Kithurst Hill to enter a tree-lined path. Turn left beside the farmhouse. The bridleway soon decides to re-climb the Downs, so turn right to pass the isolated house at Coldharbour. The pitch of its roof indicates the probability of an earlier covering of thatch.

Continue around the edges of the next field to reach a footbridge. Cross to an enclosed path that leads to the edge of the village development. Go right along the drive and turn left across the front of the Roman Catholic church to enter the car park. A stile beside the wall gives access to a field with several paths: follow the wall into a churchyard, then turn left along a twitten that leads to the main road, a right turn is needed for the village centre.

There are several inns and cafés in Storrington – whatever your choice return to the **White Horse Inn** and walk through its car park and the neighbouring White Horse Court. Another unsigned twitten leads to Browns Lane: turn left and continue along Meadowside to an open area on your left. Step right to reach a signpost beside blocks of garages. Cross Chantry Lane and enter woodland to the rear of the mill. Leave the trees over a footbridge and wander across fields to join a rutted track to **Sullington**. The road keeps to the left of the farm buildings.

After exploring the village, walk towards the Downs. The track usually has several puddles, but it redeems itself with a concrete surface as it climbs past a reservoir. As you are lifted above Hill Barn your eyes focus on another barn outlined on the skyline: remain on the now chalky track to meet the South Downs Way a few yards to the left of it. Turn right along the Way and in a little over $\frac{1}{2}$ mile you will regain the start.

POINTS OF INTEREST:

White Horse Inn – The inn sign has changed several times over the years. An old photograph from the 1920s shows the horse facing the road and greeting passers-by. In the 1970s he was disillusioned and only presented his rear end to the traffic. Now he is a steeple chaser and, complete with rider, he tackles a hurdle. Where will he be looking when you pass by?

Sullington – A farm, manor house and church is the totally integrated unit village of Sullington, the church once forming part of the house and farmyard boundary. The 115 foot tithe barn, built in 1685, is reckoned to be the finest example remaining in Sussex. In the mainly 13th-century church is a marble effigy of a knight dressed in chain mail. It is believed to be Sir William de Couvert who was the Lord of the Manor. The crossed legs are indicative of a Crusader. The heavy damage to the head, arms and legs is attributed to the reformation.

REFRESHMENTS:

The White Horse Inn, Storrington.

There are also numerous other possibilities in Storrington.

Walk 6　　　THE OUSE VIADUCT　　　4½m (7km)

Maps: OS Sheets Landranger 198; Pathfinder 1268.

A short walk to view this Victorian structure.

Start: At 334287, the Ardingly Reservoir car park.

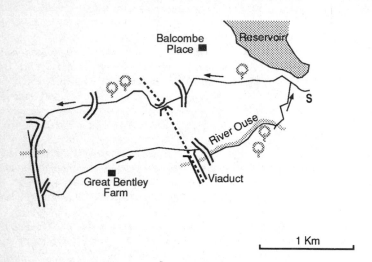

Walk up to the **reservoir** dam and take the path that leaves behind the boathouse to enter a narrow belt of trees. Go half-left in the field: as you climb, the dual arms of the reservoir become apparent. Edge along a small wood to get your first view of the viaduct. Join a concrete track and pass a pair of brick-faced cottages with a bulging timber framed first floor. The large green house on the right is Balcombe Place. Keep outside Stonehall and cross the lane to reach a farm bridge over the railway.

Turn right along the field edge, first going along the top of the cutting, then down beside a wood to reach a bridge. Now walk up to a pair of metalled signposts pointing the way over the road. Continue through the farm to reach a narrow single track lane. Turn left, thankfully the road is quiet for it is over ½ mile before you can leave the tarmac at the next junction. Turn left along the Great Bently Farm drive and just prior to the buildings break left over a stepped stile. Keep to the hedgerow on a raised section of the field, then slide off to reach a substantial footbridge over the River Ouse. Go half-right to the next farm (Ryelands) and turn right off the drive to reach the end of the **viaduct**.

Turn right along the road to reach a stile just beyond the bridge. Go over and follow the river bank to where a black pipe carries something across the stream. A wood tries to push you into the water, but gives up before you cross a final pair of footbridges. Make one more climb up a bank and the car park is just below.

POINTS OF INTEREST:

Reservoir – The Ardingly reservoir, when full, holds 1,000 million gallons and has a shoreline of over 6 miles, but there are rights of way only along short stretches. Beside the usual recreational facilities there is, to the north of West Hill causeway, a conservation area with no public access. The old Roman road from London to Brighton was submerged when the reservoir was created. Also below the waters is an old forge which was active from 1570 to 1660. It is believed that the iron tombstones in Ardingly churchyard originated from this site.

Viaduct – The Balcombe viaduct on the main line from London to Brighton was built between 1839 and 1841. In spite of having heavy continuous use, no major rebuilding has been needed and the outline remains 'as built'. It is 1,475 feet long and has 37 piers. These are unusual in that they are arched both top and bottom. When viewed through them, the structure seems endless. The Ouse Navigation, which 150 years ago was deeper and wider than today, was used for conveyance of the materials needed. Eleven million bricks were used, the majority imported from Holland and Belgium into Newhaven, then barged up river to an adjacent wharf.

REFRESHMENTS:

None on the route, but there are numerous possibilities in nearby Haywards Heath.

BRIGHTON'S BACK YARD   4¹/₂m (7km)

Maps: OS Sheets Landranger 198; Pathfinder 1307 and 1288.

A short walk on the slopes below Dyke Hill.

Start: At 274093, the Boundary Halt car park.

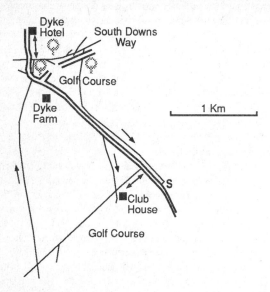

The car park is situated virtually on the county border so it just requires a step to the right to enter West Sussex. Stay on the grass beside the road, then cross into the access road for the Brighton and Hove Golf Course. There is another wide verge to keep you away from the traffic.

A few yards beyond the club house the line of the old **Dyke Railway** crosses: up hill it is marked only by lines of scattered bushes, while to the left it forms part of a surfaced cycle way dividing two golf courses. Keep ahead, going over a stile and following a field edge down to a small constructed pond. Climb past a small pit, now used as a rubbish tip, then turn right between fences to start a steady ascent. As you near the road you lose the left-hand fence. Before crossing the road, look back to trace the line of the railway: from the terminus at Dyke Farm it falls gently between bushes, provides the divider between the golf courses, then disappears behind Round Hill.

Cross the road and go straight ahead on another roadside path that leads up to the South Downs Way. Refreshment seekers must continue on the road for another 300 yards to the Dyke Hotel. Return to this point. The route goes right, through the scrub. Keep to the Way, and at the third path to the right step to the road. As a check, this is where you can see through the mouth of **the Dyke**.

The continuation path, crossing another golf course, is signed to the left. White marker posts, each with a red band, steer you between the greens to reach the next road. Here you have a choice: either go left, walking beside the road back to the start, or cross and amble down the surfaced cycle trail to the **clubhouse**. There, bear left back to the start.

POINTS OF INTEREST:

Dyke Railway – The tourist orientated Dyke Railway ran from 1887 until 1939. Traffic on summer weekends and during holidays was good but at all other times patronage was poor. To increase business various intermediate halts were added to the basic stations, though the only one of interest was for the golf course. During construction of this open platform the skeleton of a woman with a necklace of precious stones was unearthed.

The Dyke – The majority of visitors who have 'been to the Dyke' in reality never venture into the steep coombe but remain on Dyke Hill. The view across the Weald from here is superb.

The area around these hills were once a hunting ground for the Great Bustard, greyhounds being used to catch this large bird.

Clubhouse – The golf clubhouse was only 50 yards from the railway, and in 1895 an arrangement was made so that a bell would ring when the starting signal at the Dyke was pulled off. This gave the members time to finish their drinks. After World War II, the remains of the terminus station were cleared and Dyke Farm was built on the site.

REFRESHMENTS:

The Dyke Hotel, which also has a café.

Walk 8   STOPHAM   5m (8km)

Maps: OS Sheets Landranger 197; Pathfinder 1287 and 1267.
A stroll to the hills above the Upper Arun.
Start: At 026189, the green beside Stopham Church.

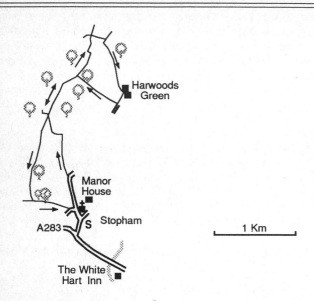

Stopham comprises a manor house, a church and a cluster of houses just off the A283, 1¹/₂ miles west of Pulborough. As this walk is mainly on bridleways it is very suitable for walkers who have difficulty in negotiating stiles. There is but one.

From the west side of the green, take the road leading northwards towards the hills. After passing a lone house currently named the Old Shop, take a bridleway on the left which climbs gradually through fields to join another at the corner of woodland. Turn right, and keeping to the right on the main track, climb steadily through chestnut woods. Where the gradient levels, the path bears right, then left before dropping steeply. Cross a footbridge and climb up out of the woods. Bear left along a field edge (here, in Spring, the woods to the left are carpeted with wild daffodils and bluebells), to reach a junction of paths in the corner of the field. Pause here a while to catch your breath and to enjoy the panoramic view of the Downs.

Turn right through gaps in the trees, where an opposite view of the Greensand hills above Dorking is revealed. Go through a gate and turn right again on to a bridleway which drops gently towards the farm at Harwoods Green. In early summer the song of resident nightingales can be heard here. Beyond the farm the track becomes a metalled road. Continue to a solitary oak and take a footpath on the right which rises, again in woodland, to meet the outward path.

Turn left and retrace your steps, but where you first entered the woods, continue straight ahead down a flower-congested green lane. At the bottom of the lane an avenue of poplar trees bear witness to earlier estate arboriculture: go past semi-derelict farm buildings and follow the track straight ahead past further stands of **coppiced chestnut**. The bridleway now turns left to join a road: continue ahead for a few yards to return to the start.

POINTS OF INTEREST:
Stopham – The Manor House is a stone built farmhouse dating from the 15th or 16th century. A stained glass window in the Norman church is dated 1638 and is reputed to have been taken from the Manor House when it was re-furbished in the 17th century.
Coppiced chestnut – This area of Sussex is well known for its chestnut coppices. Cutting of the trees is usually undertaken in the late autumn, the trees are cut to within a foot of the ground. The branches are trimmed and the bark removed, then they are left in the open to season. The end product is known as Cleft Fencing, and is popular for enclosing sizeable parcels of land. It takes about eight years for a felled area to regenerate.

REFRESHMENTS:
The White Hart, Stopham Bridge, Pulborough.

Walk 9   THE GOODWOOD TRUNDLE   5m (8km)

Maps: OS Sheets Landranger 197; Pathfinder 1286 and 1305.
From the summit of St Roche's Hill down to Chichester Plain.
Start: At 879114, the Triangle car park.

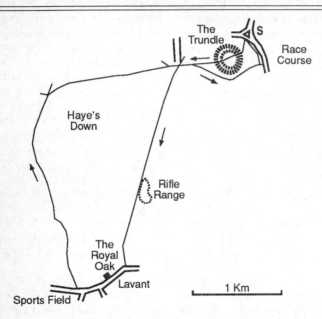

From the car park, cross the road and climb the obvious path that rises to the left of the two radio masts on **the Trundle**. Once inside the camp follow the path between the trig. pillar and third mast, but rest for a while to enjoy the 360° view that the hill offers. This is probably the best view in Sussex: the northern skyline is dominated by the heavily wooded South Downs – only through the Cocking Gap can another range of hills, above Midhurst, be viewed. The English Channel reigns over the southern arc, whilst below, your eyes are drawn to the emerald turf of 'Glorious Goodwood'. Walk off the hill through gates to another car park and take an unsigned byway that drops steadily towards Chichester. Behind a line of trees lies the **Goodwood** Terrena, and with glasses it is possible to follow the progress of the light aircraft as they practise their circuits from its airstrip. The snarl of motor engines also wafts up, for this was also once a motor circuit and is still used for testing.

Below a clump of bushes, and worked out chalk pit which houses a rifle range, the land levels. The views expires: only Bow Hill remains to the west across prairie like fields. On reaching a road, turn right among traditional flint houses and walls intermingled with more modern materials which make up Lavant. Go past the Royal Oak, continuing past the church and going over a bridge. Turn right into Sheepwash Lane, walking alongside the weed-choked **River Lavant**. Opposite the cricket pitch turn right again, going over an accommodation bridge and along a bridleway that follows the valley bottom for over $1\frac{1}{2}$ miles. The earthworks across the fields are not historic – they are the remains of a now extinct railway that ran into Midhurst. Go through a gate to a cross path and turn uphill. The going is steep at first, but becomes more friendly as you progress along a field edge back to the car park below the hill. From here either recross the Trundle, or, at the first gate, take the bridleway that contours around below the hill top. This path gives an excellent extended view across to the coast before descending on a greasy track to the road. Turn left and walk, on grass, back to the start.

POINTS OF INTEREST:

The Trundle – St Roche's Hill, or the Trundle, as it is more usually known, is an ancient hill fort. Both Neolithic and Iron Age folk lived here and it was used by both the Celts and Romans because of its dominant position above Chichester Harbour. In the Middle Ages a chapel dedicated to St Roche was erected on the summit, but on a more macabre note, a gallows also once crowned the top. One of the notorious Hawkhurst gang of smugglers ending his life there.

Goodwood – Racing at Goodwood was started by the first Duke of Richmond, but it was the third Duke who laid out a course on the Downs in 1802. The first grandstand was built in 1842. Although racing now takes place throughout the summer the main meeting – Goodwood Week, the last week of July – still features strongly in local traditions. For example, it is only then that spring cabbage seed for next years crop should be sown.

River Lavant – The river is an intermittent chalk stream, drying up for seasons or even years at a time. Born near East Dean, it stutters through Chichester to end its life in the harbour above Apuldram. Viewed from the hill above, the valley gives the impression of being 'dry'.

REFRESHMENTS:
The Royal Oak, East Lavant.
There is a mobile snack bar and ice cream van in the car park during the summer months.

Maps: OS Sheets Landranger 197; Pathfinder 1286.

A shortish hilly walk through countryside once worked by the famous Charlton hunt.

Start: At 897114, the Counters Gate car park of the Goodwood Country Park.

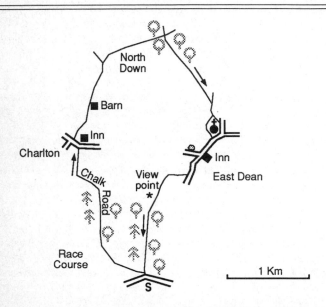

This walk has the easiest of starts for the first section is all downhill. Leave the car park at the Goodwood (western) end, cross the road and take the left-hand track beside the race course. This is the track used each morning by the second Duke of Richmond en route from his home to the **hunt** in the village below.

Join the road in Charlton opposite the **Fox Inn** and turn left to the cross-roads. Turn right into North Lane. The bridleway designation soon becomes apparent for the tarmac surface degenerates into flints. Surprisingly, the width of the road is maintained as it winds its way along the valley floor. By an iron gate, climb beside, not among, bushes and at the next stile bear away half-left following an indistinct track across to woodland. At a crossing path, turn right to leave the wood, continuing along the edge before striking down towards the, as yet invisible, village of East Dean. An aiming point for this cross-field path is an electricity pylon high on the skyline. Join a bridleway and follow it down to a road. Turn right, then right again to reach the Hurdlemakers Inn.

Almost opposite this free house is the village green, complete with pond and weeping willow. Unfortunately the green is used for the annual Guy Fawkes celebrations, the bonfire scar remaining throughout the year. From the pond follow the Goodwood road uphill, and at the village sign turn into fields. In the second field angle left, going steeply upwards to more woodland. Before crossing a stile, pause and look back over the village: the view is marred only by power lines. Now follow the pleasant woodland path back to the start.

POINTS OF INTEREST:

Hunt – In the 18th century the Charlton was the most prestigious hunt in the country surpassing both the Quorn and the Melton Mowbray. Founded in the 1670s by the Duke of Monmouth it was the economy of the area. At its zenith 150 horses were stabled around the village. The hunt's most famous day was on 26 January 1738 when a fox was found at 8.15 am and the run continued for 10 hours. It is said that 22 riders started the chase but only 3 finished, one being the Duke of Richmond who was on his fifth horse.

Fox Inn – The Fox is the only relic of the area's sporting past. However, in November 1915 the inn hosted the inaugural meeting of the Womens Institute in this country.

Both of the villages visited on this walk are estate communities, the Goodwood coat of arms being mounted on the front wall of the flint cottages opposite The Hurdlemakers in East Dean.

REFRESHMENTS:
The Fox Inn, Charlton
The Hurdlemakers Inn, East Dean.

Walk 11   ARUN VALLEY WALK II   5m (8km)

Maps: OS Sheets Landranger 197; Pathfinder 1287 and 1306.
A shorter walk through Amberley Gap.
Start: At 026118, Amberley railway station.

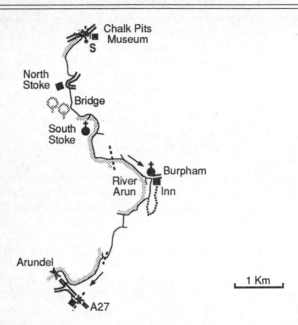

The railway can be used to return to the start of this linear walk.

Walk down to the road, go under the railway and take the path that leaves between the two **river bridges**. Turn right along the bank. Between sluices the path turns away from the river to follow bushes and drainage ditches to a road. Turn right for North Stoke. Go over a stile to the left of a telephone box on to a path that leads down to a small scale Golden Gate suspension bridge, then turns into a scrubby area, luckily keeping a couple of feet above the swamp. Rejoin the river a little to the north of South Stoke: the distance between these Stoke farmsteads is ¹/₂ mile by path, but by motorised transport a road journey of over 7 miles is needed.

Cross the bridge if you wish to visit the church and over-barn community hall, then return to continue the walk along the east bank of the river. Just prior to the railway, the Offham Cut veers away: the path, however, follows the old river, now only a backwater. Cross a couple of stiles beside a ruined building then slope away to an obvious path leading up between bushes to a junction. Turn left (unsignposted) to **Burpham** and the George and Dragon. From the inn, walk through the sports field to the children's play area from where a fenced path continues on the top of the earthworks before stepping down Jacob's Ladder to the river. Cross a double sided footbridge, then, at the next fence, you have a choice. Water babies may wish to follow the river, others bear left towards the white cottages. At the crossing path turn right then slant left to a line of poplars. A tree-lined path now drops you beside another white house.

Go over the railway to rejoin the river and follow it to Arundel. Those bound for the station turn left beside the farm buildings then left again at the road. For the town, continue along the bank, now strewn with mooring jetties. This is not the most attractive entry to the town for the river traffic uses the bank as a rubbish tip. Turn left into a hotel yard to arrive at Arundel Bridge.

POINTS OF INTEREST:

River bridges – The caravan site above Houghton Bridge covers the quay area of an old chalk quarry. Here coal was de-barged and the resultant lime exported both up and downstream. The arrival of the railway largely killed this traffic for extensive sidings were built at Amberley station. The quarry, owned by the Pepper family, was a large employer of local labour, at one time it found work for over 100 men. Today, the 36 acre site is home to the Chalk Pits Museum, largely an open air site for the display of historic industrial machines. The museum offers a superb day out.

Burpham – The village derives its name from the Saxon 'burh' or earthworks. The cricket and sports field is centred on a Saxon fort built by King Alfred. Shaped as a figure of eight it is one of four constructed in Sussex to guard against Viking raids along the tidal rivers. Today the river is a sidewater that flows beneath the village, the main stream using the 'Offham Cut', a few fields to the west.

REFRESHMENTS:
The George and Dragon, Burpham.

Walk 12 FLIGHTPATHS TO FOOTPATHS 5m (8km)

Maps: OS Sheets Landranger 198; Pathfinder 1307 and 1306.

Contrast the activity surrounding Shoreham Airport and the tranquillity of Coombes.

Start: At 206057, the parking area on the Shoreham Airport perimeter road.

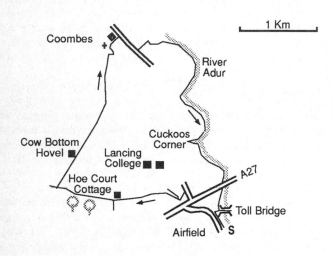

Return along the **Airport** perimeter road to the A27 and use the pelican to cross this busy road. Turn right, then, after a few steps, left into the road signposted 'Coombes'. Go left again along the driveway to Lancing College. At the end of the private roadside parking area, bear left up a bridleway. Look left for a bird's-eye view of the airport and adjoining water meadows: Hoe Court Cottage is under sentence of death as the preferred route of the Worthing by-pass aims to obliterate it. Continue to climb through scrub, then cross a stile, to the right, and traverse open fields. Looking right down the valley, your eyes are drawn to the Shoreham power station chimney and the river bridges. A notice warns against crossing Lancing Hill when the College rifle range is active. Now drop steeply to Cow Bottom Hovel. Climb again along a now-fenced path and cross a farm track to walk in open downland fields high above the river. Zig-zag down to the church and farm at **Coombes**. Picnic benches are provided in the field below the church, here you can relax and enjoy your snack.

Follow the farm drive to a road, noting the ancient petrol pump still residing in the hedge. Turn right along this quiet lane for 300 yards, then cross a stile, on the left, beside metal gates, to follow an unsigned permissive path beside a dyke to the river bank. Turn right to follow the River Adur. Before the road bridge is reached the path slips away from the river temporarily to cross a small tributary stream at a parking spot known as Cuckoos Corner. Shortly after passing under the road bridge you meet the old wooden toll bridge. Now carrying only bridleway traffic this provides a pedestrian access to the pleasures of Shoreham. Turn away from the river for a few yards, then return left on what is now the sea wall to return to the start.

POINTS OF INTEREST:

Airport – Shoreham Airport, owned by a consortium of local councils, is one of the earliest established airfields in the UK still to survive. The first commercial freight flight took off from this field in 1911, making a short hop along the coast with a cargo of light bulbs. Although scheduled services no longer operate, light aircraft utilisation is on the increase and the airport is home to the Sussex police helicopter. Both the terminal building and the globular gunnery dome have attained listed building status and the D Day Aviation Museum moved here in 1994.

Coombes – Over the years the settlement at Coombes has contracted: the church, mentioned in Domesday, was reduced in 1724. The wall paintings are believed to be the work of the same group of artists who produced those at Hardham. Entry to the churchyard is via a Tapsell gate, a device hinged on a central pivot. The farm has an enlightened attitude to agricultural education. Visitors are welcome and school visits arranged. The tractor tours of the farm being extremely popular.

REFRESHMENTS:

Nothing on the walk, but Shoreham Airport has a restaurant and bar.

Walk 13   WARNHAM   5m (8km)

Maps: OS Sheets Landranger 187; Pathfinder 1246.

A short easy walk to a deer park and farm.

Start: At 166319, Redford Avenue, Horsham.

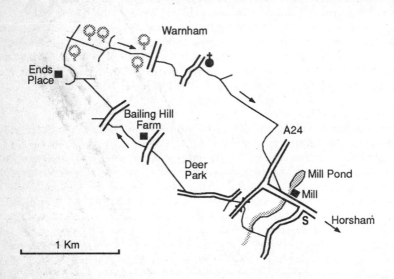

Beside the telephone box (opposite Spencer's Place) a path leads through bushes to a footbridge then on to a more substantial bridge over the Red River. Turn right at the metalled farm road which conveniently passes under the A24. Continue along Robin Hood Lane and, opposite a wood, enter the deer park. A series of black and white posts mark the route. Cross the road into Bailing Hill Farm and go between the pond and the farm house to enter the deer paddocks. The animals are reasonably tame but notices ask that you do not approach them. At the top of the rise go left beside the trees, then leave the farm beside a paling fence. Turn right at the road, passing old cottages and a converted chapel. Opposite the garages go over a stile on the left. Cross the field to the left-hand tree of a group of seven and continue to a drive. Turn left to the entrance to Ends Place, then right between the ornamental ponds. Go right into a wood, trespassing a little by keeping above the wet right of way, the bed of an intermittent stream.

At a crossing path, go right following a line of trees. Cut the corner off a field and continue towards Warnham. Do not take an inviting grass path dropping to the right: instead, go ahead through bushes. Lucas Road leads to a sports field: go round to the right of the cricket pitch and at the village hall car park turn left to the main road. The Sussex Oak is just 200 yards to the left. The path beside the church skirts the burial ground then follows a fence before breaking half-right to run between fences on the outside of the deer park. Turn right on the old road, then left into a ride through a new plantation. Cross the A24 with care and go diagonally across a field to the **Nature Reserve** parking area. Go left to a path opposite the **mill**. This follows the river bank back to the outward route.

POINTS OF INTEREST:

Nature Reserve – The Warnham Nature Reserve, open to the public in summer, includes the mill pond and land to the west. The residents of Horsham were given to understand that the reserve also included land between the Red River and the A24, land through which they have open access. This area is now to be developed as a council golf course. Due to poor public relations it appeared that Horsham District Council were to be the first authority to de-classify a nature reserve. Although the HDC were correct on a legal technicality the locals are concerned that their freedom to roam will be restricted.

Mill – Centuries ago the Red River exposed a seam of iron ore in its valley. The spoils from the open cast workings were used to dam the stream and create the pond. The mill at one time contained two waterwheels which powered the furnace bellows, its history as a foundry auxiliary was short lived for by 1700 it had been converted to grind corn. Three of the old millstones are still on display parked against the mill frontage.

REFRESHMENTS:

The Sussex Oak, Warnham.
Horsham has all the facilities of a market town.

Walk 14   RUSPER AND FRIDAY STREET   5m (8km)

Maps: OS Sheets Landranger 187; Pathfinder 1247 and 1246.

A short circuit around this border village.

Start: At 205374, the Parish Council car park.

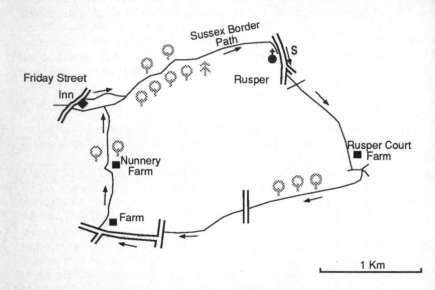

Walk through the village, keep to the right of the Star Inn and, in 20 yards, at the end of the cottages turn left. The path crosses the inn car park then runs to the rear of the houses. Continue between stables and sloping paddocks to reach a double stiled plank bridge. Continue to Rusper Court Farm and its access road.

On meeting a crossing track, go left, then turn sharp right across the face of 'Murrels' to join a hedgerow. Go right again and at a gap cross to the sunny side to follow a sporadic line of trees along the ridge to a road. Cross and continue through fields which, at first, are poorly drained but dry out as progress is made.

Cross to a footpath that slides past Donnybrook. Bisect the next field, first walking to a solitary oak, then taking the same line to a roadside power pole. Turn left along a single track lane for 20 yards, then, at a junction, go right. At the next junction go right again, along a farm drive. Leith Hill Tower and the hills above Dorking show prominently ahead to your left.

Skip left into a field at Nunnery Farm and dip towards a belt of trees. On your right the white face of The Nunnery, in over manicured grounds seeks attention. Climb out of the trees and cross the field beside an extended line of power poles. At the hedgerow (by the second pole) turn left for Friday Street. The Royal Oak is a few steps to the right. About 60 yards along the road, beyond the inn, a Sussex Border Path sign indicates the homeward route. Follow this trail to the left-hand hedge of Porters Farm, then cross and go down to enter woodland beside an old farm bridge. This section of the walk, in the trees, following a stream and a field edge path, should be peaceful, but a procession of departing aircraft from Gatwick ensure that you keep awake.

Return to the wood and drop nastily to a choice of footbridges. Slip out of the ghyll and continue left. When, finally, you emerge from the trees, follow a retained grass path across a cultivated field to a sports ground and, beyond, **Rusper**.

POINTS OF INTEREST:

Rusper – The house, Averys, opposite the Star Inn was built around 1550 and was originally known as Owensland. Until the early 19th century it was the home of the village blacksmith. Improvements and renovations were made by John Avery (hence the modern name) who divided the property and leased it to several different rural traders. After the local mill burnt down the miller installed steam driven equipment into a barn at the rear. The Plough Inn is a 15th-century house which once served as an annexe hospice run by nuns who offered passing pilgrims shelter, food and drink. The original Benedictine nunnery was demolished in 1781. When additions to the present 19th-century building were made several graves were unearthed. These were believed to be of a prioress and several sisters. Brooches, rings, a crucifix and pewter cups were also found. A tablet on the south wall of Rusper church commemorates the re-interment.

REFRESHMENTS:
The Royal Oak, Friday Street.
The Plough Inn, Rusper.

Walk 15 **BOLNEY** 5m (8km)

Maps: OS Sheets Landranger 198; Pathfinder 1268.

Leave the Brighton rat run for a short walk in quiet countryside.
Start: At 263225 a lay-by on the A272, just west of the Brighton
trunk road.

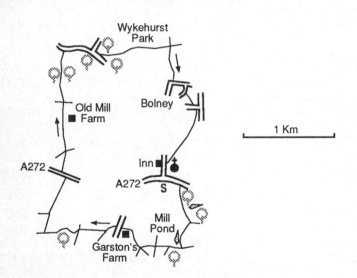

The A272 is a busy road: with care, walk back towards the Brighton road and take the
wide headland path to the right, beside the wood. Enter the trees to join a track that
passes a pond. At a junction, fork right to walk alongside another stretch of water to
the site of the now demolished Bolney Mill. Turn right and ignore all side or crossing
paths to reach **Garston's Farm**. There, follow the drive around to a lane.

    Cross and, keeping right of the next farm, shake hands with an electricity pylon.
A glance left will reveal two lines of these monsters disfiguring the view towards the
Downs. Continue ahead, then circle around a small copse hiding a slime-covered pit
to a reach a house drive. Turn right and follow this to the A272. Cross, with care, and

go left to reach a metalled farm access track beside an estate lodge. Rise gently to reach the farm shop and the Orchard Tea Rooms. Adjacent to these is a children's farm.

To continue, keep going uphill. The metalling ends beside the farmhouse – note the decorative tiles on the barn – from where the path becomes tree-lined, but continues to climb beside more orchards. Cross a small field to join a narrow lane. Turn right, and, a few yards beyond a junction, go left around the edge of a private garden before entering another wood. In Wykehurst Park, go half-left to reach a pair of pines, then continue to a bridge with an ingenious mid-span barrier. Climb up to a pylon and a fenced path that takes you out of the park.

Turn right down a sunken path down to the edge of **Bolney** village. Go left on Top Street, then right into Cherry Lane. A path jumps behind the houses and crosses a couple of fields to another lane. Bear left for a few yards, almost to the junction with the old A23. As the well-used path on the right rolls towards the village school there is a good view of the traffic hurtling towards London on the new dual carriage way. Go right to reach the churchyard and the Eight Bells. Turn left from the church gate, or right from the inn back to the A272 and the start.

POINTS OF INTEREST:

Garston's Farm – The farm contains a selection of Sussex Barns. There is a large black wooden affair, Victorian constructions and, facing you as you approach, the gem, a brick and timber frame that dates from 1475. One part of the farmhouse is even earlier, dating from around 1390.

Bolney – Bolney is a straggly village blighted by the continuous noise from the Brighton road. The local hostelry, the Eight Bells, gets its name from the peal of the church opposite. The inn sign is unusual in that it consists of a frame of eight real bells.

The church lych gate is a substantial affair, a double entry divided by a high stone bench with a decorative cross set into the top. Just the correct height for weary pall bearers to rest their burden before entering the church.

REFRESHMENTS:

The Orchard Tea Rooms, Old Mill Farm.
The Eight Bells, Bolney.

Walk 16   FULKING   5m (8km)

Maps: OS Sheets Landranger 198; Pathfinder 1288.
A short walk from Dyke Hill.
Start: At 259111, the Devils Dyke car park.

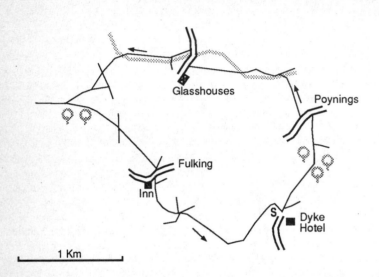

Walk to the farther end of the car park and turn left to follow a series of wooden posts.
Now select a track that will drop you steeply to a well-used path. Turn right and
contour along the face of the Downs, losing height slowly. Cross a stile and, as the
slope steepens, go down a long flight of steps to join a bridleway to the village.

At the road go left, then, at a bend, go right on a path that follows obvious baulks
towards ruined barns. Turn left at a crossing path and cross planks over a stream. Go
over stiles along the centre of a low ridge to join a narrow lane just to the right of a set
of glasshouses. Turn right for 200 yards, recrossing the stream, then going left to
accompany it through fields. Leave the stream in an open field, veering towards the
Truleigh Hill masts. Turn further to the left in midfield, by an electricity pole. On
meeting concrete the path continues ahead through a horse paddock, though it is as

easy to go left to a house and then right on another concrete track. On rejoining the line, cross a footbridge and follow headlands to the corner of a wood.

Double back left, and, as you walk beside the ditch and trees, there is a view of the scrub-capped Newtimber Hill and the more open Wolstonbury Hills. Go over the ditch and follow the path diagonally through a series of fields to reach the road at **Fulking**. The now forgotten **memorial tap and ex-fountain** is to your right, the Shepherd and Dog Inn lies just around the bend.

Now either take the track beside the inn, turning right behind the building, or step out of the garden to follow a fenced path. Either way ascends Fulking Hill. Go over a stile and continue climbing. Once clear of the scrub, continue on a wide causeway to reach a mid-point path junction. Here the Dyke Hotel complex is visible: maintain direction, passing a seat (with a fine view). At the next signpost turn left along the top of a coombe. Keep beside the faintly discernible earthwork, negotiate a final stile and veer half-right up the slope to return to the car park.

POINTS OF INTEREST:

Fulking – The village was probably the foremost centre for the South Downs sheep industry, the sheep outnumbering local residents by a ratio of in excess of ten to one. In late May or early June a convenient dip in the road by the Shepherd and Dog Inn was used as the sheep dip prior to shearing. The road was easily damned and fed by the ice cold downland stream. The dippers stood waist deep in water for days at a time. In later years some protection was obtained by standing in wooden barrels. The inn provided warmth and refreshment, though not necessarily in that order.

Memorial tap and ex-fountain – John Ruskin, the poet, stayed in Fulking for several years and it is his efforts to improve the standard of life for the locals that is honoured by the roadside 'fountain' opposite Primrose Cottage. Ruskin believed that the local stream could be harnessed to power a ram to supply village water. It was his harassment of the local company that finally led to a piped supply for the houses.

REFRESHMENTS:

The Shepherd and Dog Inn, Fulking.
The Dyke Hotel also has a café.

Walks 17 & 18   **ANGMERING PARK CIRCULARS**   5m (8km)
or 9m (14^1/$_2$km)

Maps: OS Sheets Landranger 197; Pathfinder 1306.
Two heavily wooded walks on the Downs with easy gradients.
Start: At 089069, the parking area at the northern end of Patching.

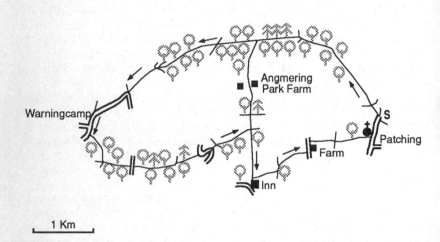

Go through the gate and take the left-hand (upper) path. Go past pathside pits and enter the trees. Go ahead on the main track, ignoring two crossing paths. The path swings left, keeping to the higher ground. At another cross path, where there is a surface improvement, turn right for a few yards, then resume the westerly direction on a forest road. Alien conifers now flank your right-hand. Dip a few feet to a junction.

The shorter route goes left here, down a grass path to Angmering Park Farm. Pass between the stables and the house, then fork left around a lone chestnut. A sloped water garden escorts you to an area of newly planted trees: where the track turns up hill, go ahead on grass, first through a smattering of trees then between fields to rejoin the longer walk.

The longer walk keeps ahead to pass an isolated house and enclosed field. The path now turns slightly left and descends gently to a meeting of five ways near the site of Jack Upperton's **gibbet**. Go through a gate and exit the trees. Half-right from here is the prominent outline of Arundel Castle. Follow the road ahead into Warningcamp. At the end of the hamlet turn left between the Old School House and a pond to re-enter woodland. Cross a stream and an inviting non-right of way, continuing amid hazel to a path junction. Turn left. Cross a lane and return to the **beech** cover, continuing for almost a mile to join a surfaced drive. On a right-hand bend fork left, signed Angmering Park. When another drive crosses leave the tarmac and go ahead. A wooden gate across the path signifies that you have rejoined the short walk.

Turn right. Run off water channels on this path uncover evidence of an earlier maintained surface, something that is sadly lacking from the lower reaches. The path finally reaches the road and the Woodmans Arms. If you visit the inn you will need to retrace your steps for 150 yards then turn right over a plank bridge. Follow a ditch to a metalled bridleway and cross left to squeeze between a copse and barbed wire fence. Strike out across a field to join a wide path between fences. Go left past a farm, then right beside silos, aiming for the houses at Patching. In the final field swing into the corner of a wood. Emerge and walk to a farm adjacent to the church. Continue to the road where a left turn will take you back to the start.

POINTS OF INTEREST:

Gibbet – Old maps of the area sited a gibbet in the woods to the west of Angmering Park, today only a copse, Gibbet Piece remains as a memory. The 18th-century coach road from Storrington crossed the Downs at this point. It was a dangerous section, the haunt of local robbers. One of these was Jack Upperton, who was caught, convicted and brought to be hanged at the scene of one of his crimes.

Beech – The truffle is a type of underground fungi greatly esteemed as a culinary delicacy. They are traced through their strong odour, the hunters normally being dogs or pigs. In the 19th century men earned a reasonable living as truffle hunters and the beech woods above Patching were a favoured location. As late as 1931 a local correspondent wrote of an Irish woman selling truffles found under Patching trees. Good sniffing!

REFRESHMENTS:

The Woodmans Arms, Hammerpot.

Maps: OS Sheets Landranger 198; Pathfinder 1288.
An energetic walk from Dyke Hill.
Start: At 259111, Devils Dyke car park.

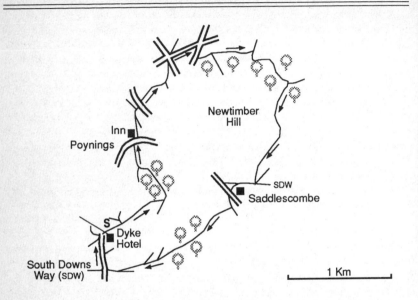

From the car park go east along the centre of the ridge and pass through the earthworks to a stile. Continue down to a second stile. Go over to meet a crossing bridleway. Turn left towards the mouth of the Dyke. Enter trees: as you approach the bottom the path becomes badly poached. There is a pedestrian only track along the top of the gully, but take care for the going is rough. Go right for **Poynings,** right again at the road, then left between the Royal Oak and its garden. Follow the concrete path to a kissing gate with an imaginative pram slide, and continue to a footbridge. Cross and walk to a road. Cross into the playground of the old school, then go past the building into fields. Go half-left through a gate to reach a garden centre sponsored roundabout.

    Take the Pycombe road for 400 yards – be careful, there is no footway or verge. At the cross-roads, turn right into a narrow lane, then left at the beginning of the trees. This is the National Trust property of Newtimber Hill. Go up the steps and follow the path signposted 'woodland'. Wind slowly upward, then, annoyingly, lose all the precious height as you drop to a bridleway. Turn right to re-ascend, still among the trees.

A gate across the path signifies the end of the climb – well almost! Break right through furze, then go right through another gate and continue to the summit ridge. Here you can look across the valley to the cars and refreshment facilities on Dyke Hill. Keep the fence on your left and, at the head of the cultivated coombe, go over a fence and head towards the settlement of Saddlescombe. Prior to meeting the South Downs Way the surface deteriorates, quite unusual on an unrestricted path. Follow the joint Way and Sussex Border Path downhill to a farm and road.

Cross left and keep to the dual designated path for a mile. It is a steep tug up to the reservoir but as you enter thorn and furze scrub the gradient eases. Ignore any side paths, but as you near the road it is possible to short cut right across to the inn. On meeting the traffic, go right: in a few yards you get probably your best view down the steep sided **Dyke**. About 200 yards more and you are back at the start.

POINTS OF INTEREST:

Poynings – The village is an ancient settlement, records dating back to 960AD. The name has evolved from this early date. Then it was Puninges; by Domesday it was Poninges. By 1370, it had become Poynnges. Sir Edward Poynings, a 15th-century Lord of the Manor, was Lord Deputy of Ireland. In 1494, he persuaded the Irish Parliament to accept English law, such that any Irish bill had to obtain prior authority from the English Privy Seal. Although known as Poynings Law the official name was The Statutes of Drogheda. They were not repealed until 1782.

Dyke – The Devil's Dyke is one of the best known features of the Sussex Downs, its closeness to Brighton being a major factor in its popularity. Legend says that this steep, north-facing coombe was created by the devil when he attempted to let in the sea and drown the churches of the Weald. Apparently Lucifer could only work at night: knowing this, a wise woman placed a candle in a sieve and displayed it in her window. Thinking it was the rising sun the devil downed tools and retreated – the Weald was saved.

REFRESHMENTS:
The Royal Oak, Poynings.
The Dyke Hotel (also houses a café).

Maps: OS Sheets Landranger 198; Pathfinder 1288.
Two fine routes, the first overshadowed by Wolstonbury
Start: At 280165, Trinity Road car park, Hurstpierpoint.

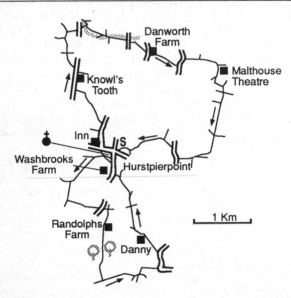

From the cross-roads beside the church, go down the Brighton Road to the 30 mph sign. Turn right. Go straight over the path junction, then, beside the third power pole, go left to a footbridge. Join a field edge track, then left on a concrete track. Beyond the farm veer back to re-cross the road. Continue on the drive to Randolph's Farm. Keep right of the buildings and follow a track into woods. Pass a cottage conversion and continue left to a belt of trees edging along the foot of Wolstonbury. Turn left. At the staggered multi-junction leave the trees (left) to swing right below **Danny**. Turn left at the road, then leave the tarmac beside a Victorian stone letterbox to enter Danny Park. The path crosses in front of the house to meet a drive. About 100 yards to the left, slip back into fields. At a junction, take the right-hand path to a belt of trees. On meeting a cross path, go right, over a stile, then ahead over one more field before going half-left into an elongated copse. Follow the farm drive to the road. Turn right for refreshments at Washbrooks Family Farm. The short walk goes left from the farm drive to the village centre.

The longer walk crosses the stile on the left. Cross a field diagonally (crossing the outward route) and walk to a road. Take the residential road beside the White Horse (1591) and enter the twitten beside No 98. Follow an estate road and cross two footbridges to reach yellow waymarks at Langton Lane. Turn right, pass the Knowl's Tooth Childrens Centre and the aptly named Long House, then depart left to a wood corner. Now head north, walking parallel to the A23. Abreast of the church, angle right to reach a hedgerow. Cross the lane, left, go over a stream and, at a junction, turn right. Keep to the raised section of the fields, cross a footbridge and follow the stream to a road. Go straight over and towards the end of the first field, slide half-right to cross the next lane adjacent to Danworth Farm.

The path could be difficult to follow in the young plantation ahead: aim to keep close to the left-hand hedge, with power cables and a college sports field to the right. At the road, go left, then turn right into the drive signed **Malthouse Theatre**. Turn right behind the theatre building, then slip across the lawn to the left of the tennis court. Take the left fork before crossing a field on a baulk line. Turn right outside the farm and go down to a footbridge. Now zig-zag left, then right. A bridleway joins from the right: it is now a longish haul, ignoring side paths, to a tree-shrouded roughish section. When the track becomes surfaced, turn right on a cross drive and right again through a wooden gate. On meeting a road, go right. Go left at the end of Alice Terrace to pass a collection of semi-residential sheds. The path is now squeezed: bear right with it, then go left through the hedge. Keep to the edge of a field, then follow the cycle sign left. Climb the steps and turn right along a road to return to the car park.

POINTS OF INTEREST:

Danny – This E-shaped, brick-built Elizabethan mansion was built in 1582. Its main claim to fame is that from here, in 1918, the terms for the German surrender were formulated by the British cabinet. One participant at the conference was a youngish Winston Churchill. The house is now divided into upmarket retirement apartments, but sections are open to the public on certain weekdays.

Malthouse Theatre – This 100 seat modern, private theatre was converted from a medieval barn. It was founded 15 years ago by the hostess of the adjoining farmhouse, who also cooks for the theatre restaurant – a converted cowshed.

REFRESHMENTS:
Cart Lodge Tea Rooms, Washbrooks Farm.

Walk 22   THE WEY ARUN CANAL   5¹/₂m (9km)

Maps: OS Sheets Landranger 197; Pathfinder 1267.

A walk along London's lost route to the sea.

Start: At 050260 – there is ample parking around the green of Wisborough Green.

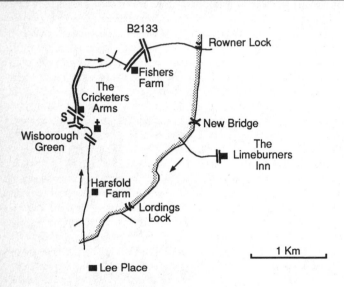

Start from the corner of the green of this cared-for village, taking the Loxwood road past the Cricketers Arms Inn. At the first corner there are two good examples of old Sussex farmhouses tiled with the local Horsham slates.

Continue along the road, then, immediately past the last house on the right, by a letterbox, take a cross field path. The path is ill-defined in the third field, so go on towards a signpost at the end of a garden fence and hedge. There, go left through a gate on to a bridleway, turn right and follow the way to a road. Almost opposite is Fishers Family Farm, worth a visit if you have children. Turn left along the road to reach the B2133. Cross and follow a bridleway, metalled at first, past Paplands Farm to reach the **Wey Arun Canal** at the restored Rowner Lock. An information board here gives an outline history of the canal and the lock restoration. Cross the canal, turn right and follow the tow path of this restored section for $^3/_4$ mile to reach New Bridge. There, cross the road and continue along the canal to the next bridge.

Here, those in need of refreshment should turn left on to a path which crosses the river, then climbs through a field and joins the driveway of Guildenhurst Manor. The **Limeburners Inn** is just to the left of the drive entrance. This diversion adds another $^3/_4$ mile to the walk. Return to the canal by the same route and continue by the now derelict or non-existent canal, going through scrubland and open fields for $1^1/_2$ miles to reach a bridleway below Lee Place. The River Arun is never too far away and at Lordings Lock traces of the aqueduct that carried the canal over the river can still be seen.

Turn right along the bridleway, following it to the road on the outskirts of Wisborough Green, passing Harsfold Farm which, along with a couple of cottages, has its own letterbox. Cross the road and take the path on the left through the churchyard. The **church** stands on a knoll overseeing the latter part of the walk and with views to the Bedham Hills – now gap-toothed courtesy of the 1987 storm. From the church it is but a few yards, passing the pond, to return to the Green.

POINTS OF INTEREST:

The Wey Arun Canal – The canal is an amalgam of the Wey and Arun Junction Canal and the Arun Navigation, meeting at Newbridge. It was authorised by an Act of Parliament in 1813 and opened in September 1816. The canal closed in 1874, although the Arun Navigation section struggled on until 1888. Newbridge wharf received its last cargo of chalk in June of that year.

The Limeburners Inn – This was originally sited at Newbridge but moved when barge traffic ceased.

Church – Parts of Wisborough Green's Church of St Peter ad Vincula are Norman, and it may have originally been a fortified keep guarding over the upper reaches of the Arun. The wall painting depicting the Crucifixion dates from the time of King John. In the Middle Ages the church was a pilgrimage centre as it contained several relics of St James. The village tapestry in the north aisle was started in 1977, took eight years to complete and shows, in three panels, interesting aspects of village life and history.

REFRESHMENTS:

The Cricketers Arms, The Green, Wisborough Green.
The Limeburners Inn, Newbridge.

Walk 23   ELSTED AND HOOKSWAY   5¹/₂m (9km)

Maps: OS Sheets Landranger 197; Pathfinder 1286.
A shortish walk over the downs, with one steep climb.
Start: At 817197, the car park beside Elsted Village Hall.

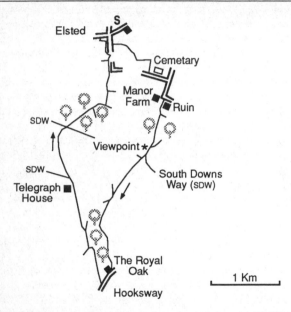

From the car park walk west to the cross-roads and turn left on to the Cocking Road. After 100 yards take the path on the left, going up a stepped bank. The path weaves through fields, firstly with a hedge to the left, going over a footbridge and then crossing a stile to go up to a road with a fence now on the right. Turn left along the road and go past a cemetery, now cared for by the **Treyford** Conservation Group. At a T-junction go right to Manor Farm. The path goes beside the farm buildings: amongst the trees to your left rest the remains of an early church. Walk towards the downs and, at a crossing path, turn left, then almost immediately right over a stile. Cross a drive then climb up to enter a wood. Follow a steep sunken track and after coming out of the trees continue steeply up a gully before veering half-left to reach an iron gate in the field corner. Pause to regain your breath and enjoy the view to the north. Blackdown, Telegraph Hill and Marley Heights are all prominent.

44

Go through the gate and turn right along a chalky track. The South Downs Way crosses: continue past Buriton Farm, going along the side of the valley among hedges overhung with wild clematis. A bridleway on the left now slopes down through a field to reach the valley bottom, from where a pleasant amble delivers you to the door of the Royal Oak Inn in **Hooksway**. From the inn, walk up the lane and opposite a cattle drinking trough, turn into a road used as a public path (RUPP) which immediately starts on a steady climb. The path is tree-lined at first, but then becomes more open. At a division, go left through a wooden gate, then along a driveway bordered by copper beech trees. Angle round to the right of Telegraph House, then leave the tarmacadam to join the South Downs Way arriving from the left. Still going uphill, follow this path as it rolls towards the col between **Beacon Hill** and Pen Hill. Where the Way turns to conquer the latter, go ahead and start to descend the tree-clad northern scarp of the Downs. When safely down, turn left on to another RUPP to reach a road. Do not go out on to it: instead, go left through a gate and follow a path parallel to the road, to reach converted farm buildings. An enclosed path now leads to a road: turn right to reach the cross-roads and walk back to the start.

POINTS OF INTEREST:

Treyford – This is a community with two cemeteries but no church. Its original 13th-century building needed heavy repair in the 1840s. However in 1849 a local benefactor deemed it necessary to have a new place of worship to cover Elsted, Treyford and neighbouring Didling. Subsequently this second church too became unsafe and was blown up in 1951. The walk passes both sites.

Hooksway – The Royal Oak is an isolated country inn, convenient for walkers and cyclists, which relies heavily on recommendations and return visits by its patrons. It was for years, when only a beer house, lorded over by Alf Ainger, a local character. From his armchair he decided if, and when, you would be served. On one occasion at a local licensing session he was questioned about his toilet facilities. The most commodious in Sussex, was his reply, five thousand acres (of woodland) out the back. The adjoining Hideaway Restaurant is open most evenings and for Sunday lunch.

Beacon Hill – The hill is topped by an ancient hill fort. Unusually this has no ramparts, the defenders obviously believing that its steepness afforded adequate protection.

REFRESHMENTS:
The Royal Oak Inn, Hooksway.
The Three Horseshoes, Elsted.

Walk 24   **COBNOR POINT**   5$\frac{1}{2}$m (9km)

Maps: OS Sheets Landranger 197; Pathfinder 1304.

*An easy walk around the Chidham Peninsula. Ideal for the winter
bird watcher.*

Start: At 793035, the Chichester Harbour Conservancy car park,
500 yards south of Chidham village.

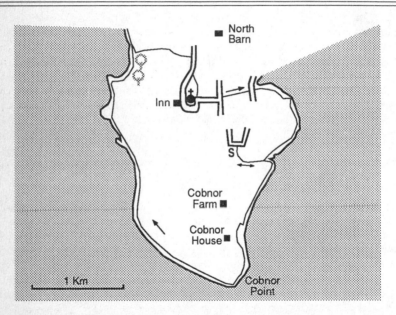

Ideally this walk should be enjoyed at different seasons of the year. In summer the
Bosham Channel is alive with all types of pleasure craft, whilst in winter the harbour
is home to thousands of waders and wild fowl.

From the car park walk up the drive towards Cobnor House and Farm. At a set of
wooden gates follow the path leftwards to the sea wall. Bosham with its accompanying
fleet of small boats lies across the channel. Continue ahead, along the wall, which
bears to the right. Just prior to a pier the path turns inland to avoid the Cobner Activity
Centre, then joins a gravelled footway for the disabled following it to a seat at Cobnor
Point. This path was opened in 1988 to allow the less able access to the shoreline.

From the seat at the Point the view is down the Chichester Channel to Hayling Island and the open sea.

Shortly after leaving the point the path steps down awkwardly to the foreshore. At high spring tides it may be necessary for the next section of the walk to be a 'trespass' along the adjacent field edge. After 150 yards, beside a wooden hut, stands a Nutbourne Marshes information board. Stay above the high water mark to pass a group of tamarisk trees and a series of oaks clinging precariously to the landside bank. At the end of a clump of thorns regain the sea wall.

This side of the peninsula is more tranquil, few boats and only the tide and sea birds for company. Take your time and enjoy this solitude. Wander for over a mile, then, beyond a larger group of thorns, turn inland to reach a road. Turn right along this unfenced lane to the village of **Chidham,** and the Old House at Home Inn.

After leaving 'The Home' follow the road around Sussex barns and flint walls, passing the church with its seemingly out of tune open bells to reach Chidham Lane. Go straight across to reach a path alongside glasshouses. At the next lane, turn left for a few yards then enter the upmarket Harbour Way. At the end of the houses a path leads from the turning circle back to the shore line. Now turn right, going either along the high water line or along the sea wall to complete the circuit. Finally, retrace your outward steps back to the start.

POINTS OF INTEREST:

Chidham – The village has always been an agricultural settlement with little interest in the sea. The soil is fertile and well suited to cereal crops, one specific strain of which was developed here. In the 1870s an attempt was made to reclaim the marshes between Chidham and Thorney Island and to convert them into agricultural land. However, the sea soon broke through the new wall and restored the landscape.

In the Second World War because of its nearness to the air base at Thorney Island, Chidham received its fair share of German attacks. One Stuka Bomber (Junkers 87) crashed at Manor Farm, which is just to the north of the walk, killing both occupants. In August 1993, aviation historians excavating the remains of the wreck discovered the wing bombs: they had laid hidden for 50 years.

REFRESHMENTS:
The Old House at Home, Chidham.

Walk 25   BOLTOPHS AND BRAMBER   5¹/₂m (9km)

Maps: OS Sheets Landranger 198; Pathfinder 1306 and 1287.
A walk off the Downs into the Adur valley.
Start: At 162095, the Steyning Bowl car park.

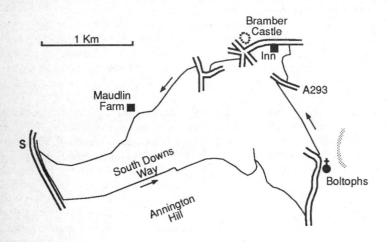

Leave the car park to follow a new section of the South Downs Way that runs south, parallel to the narrow Bostal Road. As the way continues through fields along the side of Annington Hill there are good views over Steyning, Bramber and the upper Adur. At a small plantation of commemorative beech and nursery pines go uphill for a few yards then turn left beside a wire fence. It is a circuitous descent from the hill: a few yards beyond the lone house, Tinpots, step down a water eroded bank. This path doubles back to reach a road via an old rubbish pit. Turn left for the village of **Boltophs**. The little church deserves a visit before continuing along the road. Temporarily rejoin the SDW for a few yards as it journeys across the water meadows, then turn left on to the 'Downs Link' which utilizes the old trackbed of the Horsham to Shoreham railway.

A drainage ditch accompanies the main track as it goes around to reach a road (the A293). Cross the by-pass, with care, and in the field beyond bear left towards the caravans of a mobile home park. Turn right behind the development, go over a stream and follow a drive to meet the road beside the medieval St Mary's House. Turn left to the Castle Inn, then continue to a roundabout. The road is now almost traffic free thanks to the sleeping policemen and traffic pinches. After visiting **Bramber Castle**, cross the roundabout and at the entrance to Maudlin Lane take a path down steps into a field. Keep to the right of a tennis court, then veer through farm buildings to rejoin the lane. Walk to a T-junction and turn right for 40 yards, then turn left into Sopers Lane which soon becomes a farm drive. It is now uphill all the way (well almost). The surface is good so there is no need to watch your feet: leave the houses behind and enjoy the open downland. As you climb, the semi-circular amphitheatre of the Steyning Bowl shows to the right. Backed by the Round Hill, in summer it is alive with would-be aviators and their hang gliders. Stay on the track which returns to the car park.

POINTS OF INTEREST:

Boltophs – The village is named after a patron saint of travellers, but was, for centuries, known as St Peter de Vetere Ponte (of old bridge). The bridge was probably of Roman construction, built to convey the 'tin road' from Cornwall to Pevensey. The thriving village had its own wharf, but by the mid 14th century the river and estuary was starting to contract. The settlement declined and, correspondingly, the church (to St Botolph) was reduced in size. The church floor contains many stone tablets. The majority of the inscriptions are worn away by the tread of countless feet, but one still records a date of 1683.

Bramber Castle – This was one of the five great Norman castles built to provide defence against attacks from the sea. When constructed by William de Braose it was in a superb position to control the estuary. At that time tidal waters reached the castle surrounds. Built around the same time, the adjacent church served as the castle chapel. Today only the ruined keep remains, the rest of the building falling into decay and having been used for road construction.

REFRESHMENTS:
The Castle Inn, Bramber.
St Mary's House Tea Room, (open to house visitors – summer only).

Walk 26   COWDRAY PARK   5¹/₂m (9km)

Maps: OS Sheets Landranger 197; Pathfinder 1266.

An easy, but refreshmentless, walk through parts of this well-known estate.

Start: At 887218, the North Street car park, Midhurst.

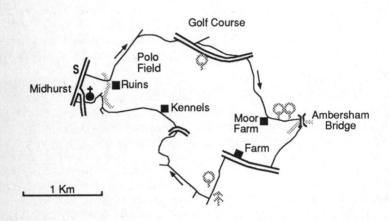

Walk down the causeway to Cowdray Ruins between meadows which at one time were flooded each winter to provide feeding areas for snipe. Just before the bridge look right to the tree covered hillock, the tunnel-like entrance there is in fact an ancient ice-hole. Cross the bridge and turn left on to a sandy track above the polo fields. Bear right beside hitching rails to reach a series of stiles and a forlorn signpost. Turn uphill to wooden gates and a road. Follow the verge downhill (right) and opposite an avenue of lime trees cross to an unmarked track, to the right of a footpath. Go through a parking area and, by keeping parallel to the road, arrive back at the road opposite the drive to **Moor Farm**. Cross, again with care, and follow the drive, with the tower and chimney stacks of the present **Cowdray House** on the right. Bear left with the drive to reach the three arched Ambersham Bridge.

Cross and follow the path on the far bank before veering across the field to join a narrow lane at a 'blasted' oak. Turn right. On a summer weekend this lane is busy with strings of polo ponies moving to the grounds at Ambersham. Pass the farm at Todham and turn left between cottages. Go over a hump and turn right through reclaimed fields with dark fen-like soil, before dropping to a T-junction. Take the right-hand track which dog-legs back to the lane at Stoney Bridge. Cross and walk to the kennels which previously housed the hounds of the Cowdray Hunt. Now follow an enclosed path which falls to a bridge over the river. Looking down at the trickle of water it is hard to imagine this as a commercial waterway, traffic only having ceased around the turn of the century. Keep close to the river before turning left up a flight of restored steps to St Anne's Hill where the foundations of the early buildings have been cleared and re-pointed. At the large pampas grass turn into an alleyway to reach the **Midhurst** church and market square. From here it is a short step back to the car park.

POINTS OF INTEREST:
Moor Farm – The unusual statues on the gate posts are believed to have been transferred in the 1920s from a Cowdray residence in London.

Cowdray House – The first house was commenced in 1492 though it was 60 years and three owners later before it was completed. Queen Elizabeth I was a visitor in 1591. The Cowdray Curse, of fire and water, came true in 1793, when within 8 days the house was gutted by fire and the last of the Montague family was drowned while attempting to shoot the Rhine falls. The ruins are open to the public each summer.

Midhurst – Mention Midhurst and one automatically thinks of Cowdray, but in fact, the houses and homelands of the title are in the neighbouring parish of Easebourne. St Anne's Hill is the site of a Norman castle. The dates of its building and demise are unknown, but with its superb location overlooking the river it is unlikely that it was the first fort to have been erected here. When exploring Midhurst look out for the following lanes: Duck, Sheep and Wool. It was via these different thoroughfares that the farm produce was steered to the market – an early attempt to regulate traffic flow.

REFRESHMENTS:
None on the walk, but many choices in Midhurst.

Walk 27   ASHINGTON AND WARMINGHURST   5¹/₂m (9km)

Maps: OS Sheets Landranger 198; Pathfinder 1287.

A short walk in an area with strong early American connections.

Start: At 129159, Ashington Church.

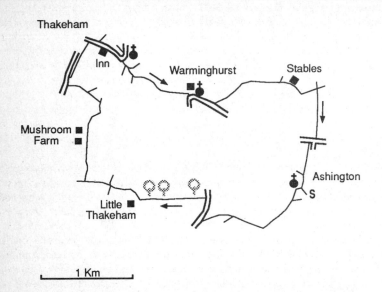

Walk along a concrete track for 20 yards then go left over a stile beside a high Leylandii hedge. Join a path from the houses and cross a field to a gate to the right of the red-roofed barn. Turn right along a track to a road. Go right for 300 yards, then climb left up the bank to reach a field-edge path beside two bands of trees. Slide down (a rope is usually available for assistance) and diagonally cross the field below **Little Thakeham**, recognised by tall chimneys. Follow the wire fence to a junction of paths at a double gated lane end. Maintain direction along the lane. Turn right opposite a farm, climb a slope, then drop down between a mushroom farm and its spent compost heaps. The path now becomes rutted as it wheels round to meet a road beside a sports field.

Turn right, go past houses and, at the end of the footway, cross through a hedge and walk above the road to reach the houses on **Thakeham** Street. Turn right down the road with its mixture of housing, modern, thatched and timber framed, from which the White Lion stands a little aloof on a bank. Walk down the Street and, beside the church, go through the white gates and, ignoring all side paths, follow a farm track through fields to **Warminghurst** where a notice on the church door asks visitors to call at the farmhouse for the key. Continue along the lane that circles to the south of the church, leaving the tarmac beside a pair of cottages. Walk through fields of horses from the riding centre to join a track that keeps to the right of the stables, and then, at a sharp bend, cross into a field. Walk beside the hedge, parallel to the track, and at a cross path turn right, aiming for the gable end of a white house. A line too far to the left will deposit you in a slurry pit! A narrow path now leads up to an estate road: turn right, then left on a tarmac path to the rear of the houses and follow it back to the church.

POINTS OF INTEREST:

Little Thakeham – The house was designed by Sir Edwin Lutyens and built of local sandstone in 1902. The gardens were by Lutyen's collaborator Gertrude Jekyll. The house is now a private hotel and restaurant.

Thakeham – In the 19th century the village was the centre of a poor law union, complete with workhouse. How things change – a few years ago when the local post office closed, BT was asked to provide a public phone box in the village. They declined, considering Thakeham to be an affluent community and believing little revenue would be forthcoming from a public phone.

Warminghurst – William Penn, the founder of Pennsylvania, and notable member of the Society of Friends or Quakers, lived here for 25 years. He and his family usually worshipped at the Blue Idol at Coolham, the Master and his wife riding there on horseback, the children following behind in an ox cart. Whilst living at Warminghurst the idea of a safe haven for persecuted Quakers was born and the constitution of the new American state was drafted. After Penn's death his house was pulled down and the present building erected. Warminghurst church, which is under the care of the redundant churches fund, contains good examples of late 18th-century box pews and a three-decker pulpit.

REFRESHMENTS:
The White Lion, Thakeham.
The Red Lion, Ashington (at the southern end of the village).

Walk 28 SLINDON 5¹/₂m (9km)

Maps: OS Sheets Landranger 197; Pathfinder 1305 and 1286.,
A short downland walk in the valleys and woods above Slindon.
Start: At 961085, the Roman Catholic Church, Slindon.

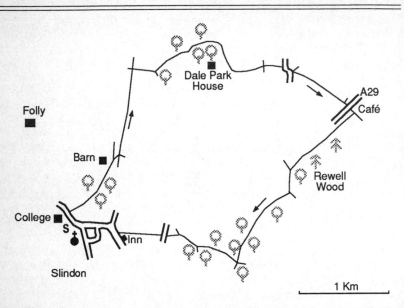

Park the car close to the wall and walk away from the village to reach the college entrance and a bridleway that leads to the Downs. At the flint barn, **Nore Folly** can be seen across the valley. From the end of the barn wall step up right to a bench seat and junction of paths. Follow the fenced track (Bridleway to Bignor) which rolls towards the radio mast on Bignor Hill. The track dips to a crossing path: turn right to the edge of a beech wood. Go through a gate and bear half-left to the corner of woodland above **Dale Park House**. Follow the flint track uphill then turn right on a metalled drive to the valley bottom. Continue uphill to a road. Turn right to the telephone box, the hub of **Madehurst**. Go ahead beside the houses: a stile behind some ivy marks the beginning of a path to the A29. Cross to the Fairmile Café.

From the café's car park follow the blue posted trail beneath yews into open downland. Where the path divides, turn uphill to reach a wood and another marker.

Climb sharply into chestnut coppices, leaving the blue trail by turning back right along the ridge. Go past a conifer plantation and slope down to a gate and unsignposted path junction. Turn right, going downhill still towards the traffic noise and the A29. At the edge of the trees, beside the entrance to a wooden building, turn left up to the road. Cross, with care, and climb steps to a path which, although not high, gives fine views over the coastal plain. Follow the path back to **Slindon**, arriving by the Newburgh Arms. Continue along Top Road, passing the post office and pottery, then turn left into narrow Dyers Lane. On meeting Church Hill, turn right back to the start.

POINTS OF INTEREST:

Nore Folly – The folly was built in the late 18th century for the Countess of Newburgh. It is based on the design of an Italian arch. It had a habitable thatched room attached and was used as a shooting lodge, but now only the arch remains.

Dale Park House – The original house was regarded as an ugly structure and was demolished in 1959, the present building being repositioned to improve the view. However, its white facade tends to impose upon the surrounding woodland.

Madehurst – In Madehurst Wood, below the conifer plantation, lurks a series of metal boundary posts. Situated only a few yards from the path they are readily visible. Each bears the letter F and N. No prizes, but how many can you spot?

Slindon – This quiet village hangs on to the southern slopes of the Downs. Owned mainly by the National Trust it has the atmosphere of a continental village. Slindon House (now the college) is built on the site of a palace of the Archbishop of Canterbury. The present building is a re-erection of a 16th-century house of which only a tower remains. Two thatched buildings are interesting: the post office is surely one of the most picturesque in the county, while the railway carriage in the grounds of Church House is certainly unusual. If the church is open, make for its southern chancel where there is a wooden effigy, unique to Sussex. Five feet in length and dressed in armour of the late Wars of the Roses period it is almost certainly that of Sir Anthony St Leger who died in 1539.

REFRESHMENTS:

The Fairmile Café, on the A29.
The Newburgh Arms, Slindon.

Maps: OS Sheets Landranger 198 and 197; Pathfinder 1306.

A short walk to the Highdown viewpoint via the less frequented northern slopes.

Start: At 096066, Clapham Church.

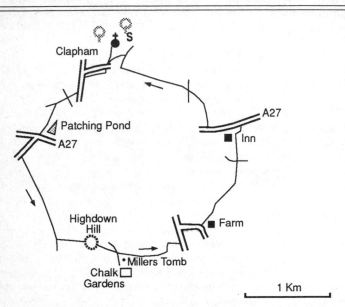

Return down the church driveway and cross The Street. Ensure that you do not miss the right turn at the end of the flint wall: this path follows garden fences to a road. Cross to the foot way and turn left for the village hall. The next path crosses the cricket field (avoid the square please), goes over a stile and turns left at the hedgerow to reach the A27 by Patching Pond. The road junction may still be in state of flux due to 'improvements' however take the Angmering road. After 400 yards take the path to the left, beside the mini sewerage works, that climbs slowly through fields to surprise **Highdown Hill** from the rear. At a high stile go left into a disused pit, then up to the trig. point and the summit earthworks.

From the information board make your way down to the gateway where you are greeted by the Worthing Council. **The Miller's Tomb** is just to the right, under the beech tree. Keep to the left of the car park for the **Chalk Gardens**, going down to a flint barn. On meeting a road turn left, then right into Titnore Way.

Turn left at a roundabout to pass beside the old farmhouse, then cross a series of plank bridges dropped into uncultivated fields. In the last field before the houses the right of way crosses half-left to the corner. The locals and their dogs seem to favour a field edge option – the choice is yours. Continue left on a grassy track that takes you to within yards of the Coach and Horses Inn on the A27.

It is only a short walk back to the start so you can take a leisurely break. When you are ready, follow the grass verge then cross, with care, into the drive of Holt Farm. At the house turn half-left across the field above the buildings. A white board on an electricity pole will guide you in the right direction. Cross the access drive and climb a stile to get the first view of the Clapham houses. On leaving the fields take the track to the right. Go left towards the farm, but immediately left again to pass behind the houses. Finally reverse the outward route along the church driveway.

POINTS OF INTEREST:

Highdown Hill – This National Trust site is crowned by an early Iron Age fort dating from about 500BC. The excavated finds are in the Worthing museum.

The Miller's Tomb – The tomb belongs to a renowned local smuggler and eccentric miller, John Olliver, who died in 1793. For 27 years he lived with his coffin below his bed – just in case. He was interred upside down for he believed that on resurrection day the world would reverse. His funeral was planned in advance and all mourners were invited to the celebration and were instructed to wear bright and joyful clothes.

Chalk Gardens – For those who live on chalklands a visit to the Gardens is a must. Created out of a pit by Sir Frederick Stern, the Gardens contain rare plants and shrubs, collected worldwide, but all suitable for chalk soils. The Gardens were gifted to the local council in 1967. The green painted letter box at the entrance was erected by Lady Stern as a memorial to her husband. A plate on the box invites visitors to enjoy the Gardens and contribute towards their upkeep.

REFRESHMENTS:

The Coach and Horses Inn, on the A27.

Walk 30   **ASHURST**   5$\frac{1}{2}$m (9km)

Maps: OS Sheets Landranger 198; Pathfinder 1287.
An easy walk on a largely waymarked community path.
Start: At 191192, Partridge Green Village Hall.

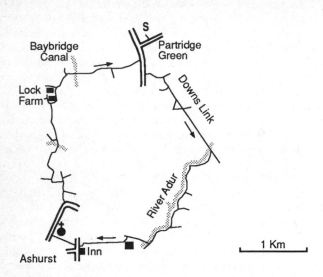

Walk beside the hall to the High Street. Turn right and go left over the old railway
bridge. The pavement for this stretch of road is on the 'wrong' side so it entails two
crossings – please be careful. A path now edges through the industrial estate to reach
the old railway. Leave the right of way and turn right on to a short stretch of
undesignated path to join the Downs Link. Here you encounter the first waymarks of
a 'Low Weald Circular Walk'. You can make good progress along this level surface.
One farmer is using this section for his attempt to enter the famous Guinness book –
the longest dung heap in Britain. In the field all traces of the railway have disappeared
apart from smudges of underfoot shingle.

Cross the river and turn right along the bank. At the junction with the old canal
two footbridges cross the waterways. At the next bridge follow the waymarkers over
the river, then walk through a couple of fields below the farm. Turn left at an oak tree

58

to reach the buildings. Walk along the farm drive to the road. The Fountain Inn, **Ashurst** is now to the left.

Cross the road to a footpath that leads directly to a lane. Turn right for the church and where the road executes a 90° turn to the right, go ahead into Ford Lane. Turn left into a farm and follow the path as it swings right over a small hillock before returning to the old road, now relegated in places to a field edge path.

Turn towards Lock Farm, keeping to the right of all the farm buildings to join a lane back to Partridge Green. The **Baybridge Canal** is crossed at Lock Bridge where a raised footway has been provided should the road be flooded. The canal cut and lock was down stream but nothing is visible from the bridge. Rejoin the main road by the railway bridge from where it is a short step back to the start.

POINTS OF INTEREST:

Ashurst – The village has a good pub, scattered houses and a church away from the main settlement. Prior to the Norman conquest, there was a chantry here, administered by the Benedictine monks of Fecamp, which may have been incorporated into the church. The church was another built by the Knights Templers, around 1200AD. Inside is an ancient vamping horn – a type of one man band for church music. Invented in the reign of Charles II the Ashurst specimen is one of only seven remaining in England.

Baybridge Canal – The canal was one of the least known and least significant waterways in the UK. Less than $3^1/_2$ miles long and totally within the parish of West Grinstead it was a canalised river navigation. Two cuts were made to house the required locks. Completed around 1826 the main cargoes carried were cereals and timber from local estates. The railway arrived, and the canal was little used after 1861, finally closing 14 years later.

REFRESHMENTS:

The Fountain Inn, Ashurst.

Walk 31   SHARPTHORNE   5½m (9km)

Maps: OS Sheets Landranger 187; Pathfinder 1247.

A high Wealden walk south of the Weir Wood Reservoir.

Start: At 386348, a small car park at the end of a single track lane north of Willett's Bridge.

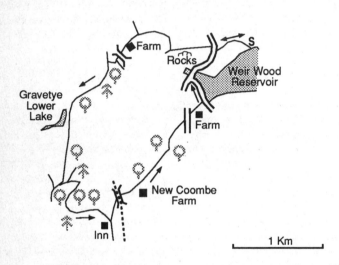

Walk back up the lane to the road and go right for 40 yards to reach a bridleway, to the left beside a stand of rocks. A few yards along the path deviate left to pass below a larger **outcrop of rocks**, popular with climbers and engravers with Valentine aspirations. Climb back up to the bridleway. Now at the first field keep right above a gully, then join a track of sorts which passes between farm buildings and goes under the old railway. Follow the drive left towards Birch Farm Nurseries.

    At the bridge turn right into a field and follow the stream beside the woodland. Now go left into the trees on an old track beside Gravetye Lower Lake. Should you wish to extend the walk the Forestry Commission have waymarked a circular stroll around the water. Leave the end of the lake, veering slightly left to reach a pinch point between two woods: large stone steps for a redundant stile confirm that you are on line. Cross a field or, if it is heavily cropped, use the headlands, to reach a stile in the top left-hand corner. Turn back beside the rubbish pits, then fork right on a wide rutted track that joins a gravelled forestry road. Turn right and walk along to the Bluebell Inn.

From the inn's door, turn left along the concrete farm drive and walk below the rebuilt bridge of the Bluebell Line extension, swinging below New Coombe Farm. As the drive bends down towards the sewerage works, strike half-right across the field. Dip into the trees, then follow yellow waymarkers, rising leftwards to enter a band of trees. Cross the road to reach an access drive and, beyond the buildings, step right into a clump of nettles and go down to join a road on the southern shore of **Weir Wood Reservoir**.

Go left to a junction. Turn right over the bridge and continue along this narrow and twisting section of road to rejoin the outward lane. Turn right to regain the start.

POINTS OF INTEREST:

Weir Wood Reservoir – Weir Wood is not an enlarged hammer pond but was created as a reservoir in 1954. It is fed by the infant River Medway. The county boundary snakes through the centre of the water obviously following the line of the drowned features. Over 280 acres in extent, the eastern half is given to leisure activities while the western end is a nature reserve. With a resident company of waterfowl it usually hosts passage ospreys for a few days whilst they are on their spring and autumn migrations. In the dry summer of the late 1980s the drowned section of Admiral's Bridge Lane re-appeared from the mud.

Outcrop of rocks – The rocks at the start of the walk are an outcrop of the ridge that extends from Balcombe through East Grinstead to Tunbridge Wells. Consisting of sandstones, the different strata have a varying resistance to the elements, hence the unusual shapes and overhangs. The largest outcrop is at High Rocks, a little to the south-west of Tunbridge Wells were there is an activity centre specialising in rock climbing.

REFRESHMENTS:
The Bluebell Inn, Sharpthorne.

Walk 32   CHAILEY COMMON   5¹/₂m (9km)

Maps: OS Sheets Landranger 198; Pathfinder 1268.

A walk across the border to an isolated area of heathland.

Start: At 369232, Scaynes Hill parish church.

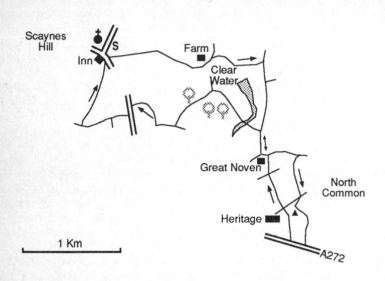

Walk up to the cross-roads and turn left across the face of a garage. Beside the shop, go into Clearwater Lane. Slowly lose height, pass a pair of cottages and, at the farm, follow the Sussex Border Path signs into fields. Meander down to a stream, then turn right on the crossing path. Follow hedgerows past a plantation of Christmas trees, go under the power lines and at Great Novan Farm turn left on a semi-concrete farm drive. Cross the county divide and turn back to Little Novan. Opposite the house go left on to **North Common**. Go over planks and try to find a path that will take you through the furze to a grassy area. As you approach the crest the static sails of the mill appear. There is a conveniently placed memorial seat sitting beside a wide ride: to its rear is the trig. point.

Take the path that runs south-east from the trig. point to a white bungalow. Continue past a house with a Woodbine sign and continue to the end of an unmade road. On reaching the A272 turn right, with care, for the Post Office which sells canned drinks and confectionery. Now walk along to a metalled drive leading to one section of the **Chailey Heritage** complex. Do not enter the school grounds: instead, break right back on to the Common to round the buildings and windmill. Re-cross the wide track and follow a slightly sunken path that steers towards Great Noven. Drop towards the trees and look for a railed fence falling from the farm. Go to this, where you will find more planks and a welcoming West Sussex signpost. Retrace your outward route through the farm and at the end of the first field turn left. Cross the causeway at the end of the totally misnamed Clearwater, then walk beside Great Wood. Dip down to a bridge, but do not cross: instead, go left, following the ruts up into a wood. There, immediately break right on an indistinct path. Leave the trees and bear left, then right at a staggered cross path. Go around the pond beside a lonely house, and follow signs to a road. Cross and go left on a footway for 80 yards to reach the horse-chestnut lined drive to Hooklands. Fork right between Old and New Cottages to follow a tree-enclosed path which emerges at **Scaynes Hill** opposite the garage.

POINTS OF INTEREST:

Scaynes Hill – The churches and schools in Scaynes Hill have over the years played a game of musical chairs. The village church was built in 1858 as a school, an educational establishment during the week converting on a Sunday to religious activities. This arrangement continued for several years, but as the population grew the school was forced to move into another building – one that started its life as a chapel!

North Common – The Common at Chailey is a 400 acre Nature Reserve consisting mainly of wet and dry heathland. The smock mill is considered to be placed at the geographic centre of Sussex. Seven mills have been recorded on this site, the earliest dating from 1595. The present incumbent started life in 1830 at West Hoathly and moved to Chailey 34 years later, continuing to operate until 1911.

Chailey Heritage – The word School is usually omitted from the title here. The school was founded in 1903 by two London social workers for East End physically handicapped children. At that time the majority of pupils suffered from TB. One of the founders, Dame Grace Kimmins, remained in charge for 50 years. From an initial start with only 7 children, this world recognised established now cares for over 200 pupils, both from the UK and overseas.

REFRESHMENTS:
The Farmers, Scaynes Hill.
The Post Office Stores, North Chailey.

Walk 33   **COPTHORNE** $5^3/_4$m (9km)
Maps: OS Sheets Landranger 187; Pathfinder 1247.
A visit to a small remaining fragment of the ancient Wealden forest.
Start: At 346375, Crawley Down village centre.

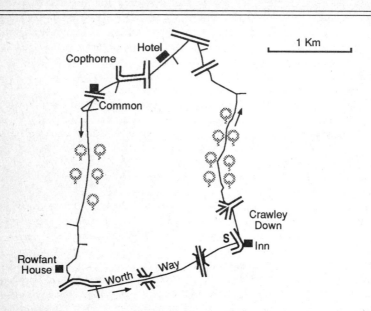

Park beside the shops, or in adjacent Old Station Close. Cross to the Royal Oak, then walk up Bowers Place, the road to the right of the Green. At the top, go right to the war memorial, then left into Sandy Lane. After 50 yards take Cottinglye Lane. At first, this is an unsurfaced track, but after turning left it collects tarmac and offers a pleasant stroll through the trees. Beside the gate to a set of low buildings (which the OS map calls The Monastery) go left into a fenced path. At the T-junction, turn left – for a look at the pond go right then return to the junction. Go over a stile, then left through a hedge gap and walk down to the corner of a wood. Follow the wood edge to another enclosed path which utilises some duckboards to reach a road.

Cross straight over and take the path beside Smugglers Cottage: a few easily missed concrete footpath tablets are now appearing. Continue to meet a road opposite the Dome Wood estate. Go left for 100 yards, then turn back into the mainly unsurfaced Chapel Lane. This track passes to the rear of a hotel that has an ongoing identity crisis. Cross a road into Mill Lane. This is the county boundary, Sussex is to your left, Surrey on your right. At the school, turn half-left into the Common continuing to arrive beside the Abergavenny Arms, Copthorne.

Cross a road into **Copthorne Common** (heading south). Although there is open access, for route finding it is best to keep to the main cinder track. Beyond the crossing path this converts into an access drive, finally being relegated to a woodland path. Continue through Home Farm, where Sussex Border Path signs appear. Drop down into trees, go around the ponds and under the arch at Rowfant House. Follow the drive rightwards to a white lodge. A look into the trees here reveals large bunches of mistletoe.

Go left along road, then right into the business centre. After 50 yards you meet the **Worth Way**. Turn left with it for a mile of level walking along an old railway back to Crawley Down. There, go up one final, artificial slope to reach the houses at the end of Old Station Close.

POINTS OF INTEREST:
Copthorne Common – Originally part of the large Worth parish, the Common was, for centuries, little more than a clearing in Ashdown Forest. Old maps show an area of rough ground surrounded by scruffy woodland. In the Middle Ages it was the haunt of smugglers, poachers, gypsies and unsavoury characters, thankful for the remoteness that the area offered. Development was slow but inevitable, today only the two sections of the common remain as reminders of an earlier age.

Worth Way – The Way is a six mile walk from Three Bridges to East Grinstead, largely following the line of the single track railway that closed in 1967. The line originally opened in 1855 with Rowfant as the only intermediate station. Several features of the old station still remain, adjacent to the county council car park. All traces of the other station, Grange Road, which was opened later are submerged beneath the row of shops in Crawley Down village centre.

REFRESHMENTS:
The Abergavenny Arms, Copthorne.
The Royal Oak, Crawley Down.

Walk 34   SUTTON   6m (9¹/₂km)

Maps: OS Sheets Landranger 197; Pathfinder 1286.

A walk off the chalk to visit a couple of peaceful settlements.

Start: At 955161, the car park on Ducton Hill.

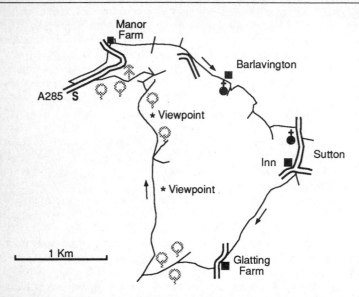

Leave the **car park** and walk uphill for a few yards before doubling back below the cars. **DO NOT** attempt the slope beside the indicator, it is lethal. The path leaves the trees to reach the A285 at the entrance to Manor Farm. Cross, with care, into the drive and turn right through an open field, keeping roughly parallel to a minor road on the right. Obliquely cross above the picturesque mill, then go straight ahead on an undulating path to Barlavington. A plethora of 'Private' signs ensure you have no difficulty in following the correct way to the church. Take a break at this beautiful spot, situated beneath a wooded coombe of the Downs.

Continue around the farm buildings before turning on to another switchback. Dip across to a stream, then turn left to join the driveway of a wooden shingled house. Go right along the road to **Sutton church** and the White Horse Inn. The village is almost traffic free, the peace disturbed only by an occasional horse or the squeak from a barrow wheel. From the inn, cross to the thatched cottage where an ancient sign proclaims – Public Footpath to Bignor. Do not cross the field: instead, turn right along headlands before breaking towards the radio masts on Bignor Hill. Follow the road around the barns at Glatting Farm and, opposite the house, strike across two fields towards woodland. Join a bridleway to continue upwards on an easier gradient.

On meeting another track, turn back right. This enclosed path finds a more level way around Farm Hill. Where a fence crosses there is a magnificent view northwards over the Weald. At the next meeting of paths, keep along the edge of the wood before climbing over the shoulder of Ducton Down where there is a bench seat and one final viewpoint, this time towards the east. Now begin the final descent of the walk. In the wood the rights of way differ from those shown on the present OS maps, so turn left at the first junction, right at the next, and first left at the third. This will bring you back to the road just a few yards below the car park.

POINTS OF INTEREST:

Car park – The car park on Ducton Hill has been provided by the Rees Jeffreys Road Fund and the direction indicator by the Automobile Association. Among the points arrowed are Torberry Hill, close to the Hampshire border; Telegraph and Older hills, both above Midhurst; Blackdown; and, away in Surrey, Leith Hill. Spend a few minutes studying their outlines for there is a better viewpoint towards the end of the walk where you will be able to astonish all with your local knowledge.

Sutton church – The church is built of local Pulborough stone. The earliest portion, the north wall of the nave, dates from the 11th century. As with many Sussex churches it was heavily restored in the 19th century. Relatively free of internal memorials, on the south wall hangs a painting by Claude Muncaster. *Sutton on a Summer Day* quietly catches the mood of these underdown settlements. The yew trees in the churchyard were planted in 1666.

REFRESHMENTS:
The White Horse Inn, Sutton.

Walk 35　　　SLAUGHAM　　　6m (9½km)

Maps: OS Sheets Landranger 198; Pathfinder 1268.

A varied walk in countryside that found favour with England's admiral.

Start: At 251281, Furnace Pond, Slaugham Common.

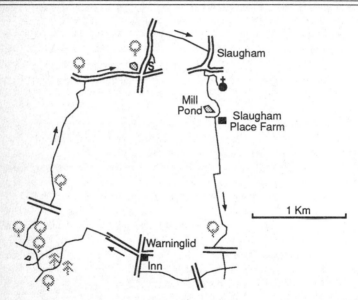

In winter the trees around the parking area contain many bird feeders maintained by a local benefactor. Walk up the quaintly named Coos Lane and take the second path on the right, 30 yards past the entrance to Phipps. The path leads to a bridge, fork right to arrive at the edge of the **Slaugham**. Turn right down Slaugham Street, pass a white phone box and an Edward VII pillar box and cross into the **churchyard**. Tombstone enthusiasts will have a field day here. There is a signpost beside the church door: keep ahead and drop down towards the mill pond. Go left around the head of the water, then right on a farm drive. Almost immediately follow a track up the slope into fields. Pass between paddocks, stepping right to rejoin the correct line. Cross to the edge of the scrub and follow a drainage ditch, bending slightly for a stile into woodland. Meander through the trees and in the field beyond go half-right to a roadside stile in front of a white building. Turn left for 150 yards then go right along the drive of Southgate Farm. At the stepped crossing path, beyond the stable block, go right. The next path leaves the lane opposite the black bungalow and delivers you to The Street at Warninglid. Turn left for the Half Moon Inn.

Leave the inn to go ahead along Warninglid Lane. At a bend, go left along a bridleway that accompanies the road before ending: drop steeply into a ghyll. Take the footpath out and beyond the refuse tip go left through a missing gate into a stand of pines. Go round and down to a path junction. Turn right and keep right to cross a bridleway. A footbridge takes you over the head of a pond: climb the slope and ignore side paths until, just prior to a series of small tarns (ponds), you strike right into chestnuts to reach a drive and road. Go right for 100 yards, then go through the right-hand of a pair of gates. Climb to the end of a band of trees and follow a bridleway that, in winter, becomes badly poached and muddy. At an isolated cottage, join a drive for a clean easy stroll to a road. Turn right along this quiet lane, it has a wide verge, and after 700 yards you will reach the pond and start point.

POINTS OF INTEREST:

Slaugham – Between the wars when villages were being 'developed' Slaugham was lucky to be under the control of a Colonel Warren who purchased the manor in 1920. One of the last Lords of the Manor in England, he believed that the title conferred duties as well as rights. He paid for the burying of the telephone wires that were disfiguring the village, obtained permission for the painting of the phone box to blend with the adjacent buildings, and as the old inn was obscuring the view of the church, had it destroyed. Slaugham Manor is now used by the Sussex police as a residential, training and conference centre.

Churchyard – There are several tombstones in St Mary's churchyard relating to the Matcham family. Nelson's sister, Catherine, married George of this involved clan. This gave Horatio an excuse to leave the London scene and continue his liaison with Emma Hamilton. It was said that he loved the countryside around Slaugham and Warninglid, but more probably he loved the secrecy and privacy that the area offered. One path, not a right of way, in the wood below Ashfold is known locally as Nelson's path – one of his love trails?

REFRESHMENTS:
The White Horse Inn, Warninglid.

Walk 36   LINDFIELD   6m (9½km)

Maps: OS Sheets Landranger 198; Pathfinder 1268.
The 'tracks' are abandoned or abortive mid-Sussex railways.
Start: At 334287, the Ardingly reservoir car park.

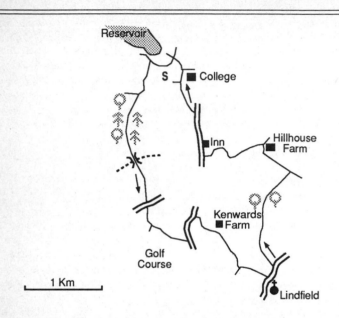

Walk up to the reservoir dam and at the boathouse turn back left along a hedgerow. From here there is a good view of Ardingly College. Drop to a pair of footbridges, then go half-right into trees. Follow the main track through mixed woods and join a farm drive to cross the old **Ardingly railway**: one set of tracks still remains. Continue ahead, going over a footbridge and passing a lonely cottage to reach a lane. On the right are the earthworks and bridge wall of a **railway that never was**.

Cross to another woodland path, then go into a golf course. Follow the signposts, going right, then left to houses and a private drive. At the road turn left. Negotiate a double bend, and then turn right along the drive to Kenwards Farm. The first section usurps the abortive railway track bed, but breaks away at a white lamp post. There is now easy walking on a well made track: go left along the back of the houses to join the main road at the end of Lindfield village. Turn right for a leisurely look round this attractive community or perhaps call in at the **Bent Arms** for some refreshment.

From the church head out of the village, turning left into Spring Lane which soon converts to a farm access road. Pass through the buildings to reach a high rise bridge over the River Ouse. An area of sedge and brambles follows. Keep left of the next hedge, then go left again along the next drive to follow the concrete track beside Hill House Farm. At the cottages there is a good case for a right of way to the north. Other parties obviously think the same for an official notice warns you off.

To compensate, a wide grass path leads forward. Squeeze behind the tennis court at Avins Farm. The drive meets the road opposite the ex-station house which is now used as offices for a roadstone company. Turn right, up the slope, passing, or calling in at, the Avins Bridge Inn and turn left into the reservoir road. This old road is now re-classified as a bridleway. Leave the amenity road and go into the rear entrance to the college. Beyond the buildings, turn left around the pond, then break left again to reach the car park.

POINTS OF INTEREST:
Railway that never was – The Ouse Valley Line was proposed as a barrier by the LBSCR against intrusion into its area by competing companies. Work began in 1865 but a year, later following a truce between the feuding parties, everything was abandoned.
Ardingly railway – The $3^1/_2$ mile line from Copyhold Junction (on the main Brighton route) to Horsted Keynes was opened in 1883 to provide an alternate access to the coast. During the Second World War it was considered so vital a link that the junction signal box at Horsted Keynes was manned continuously. Electrified in 1935, British Rail deemed it unnecessary less than thirty years later and as a final insult blew up the viaduct at the eastern end 'for maintenance reasons'. Today a single track conveys an occasional aggregate train to Ardingly.
Bent Arms, Lindfield – The inn is named after a local family but it has previously been known as the White Lion and Wichelo's (a Brighton brewer). It was an important coaching inn – when Sussex roads were poor and the drivers uncaring, resting passengers found time to nip up to the church, where in front of a dedication to St Christopher they no doubt prayed for a safe onward journey.

REFRESHMENTS:
There are several inns and a coffee shop in Lindfield.

Walk 37   BOSHAM AND FISHBOURNE   6m (9km)

Maps: OS Sheets Landranger 197; Pathfinder 1305.
A walk connecting two channels of Chichester Harbour.
Start: At 806040, Old Bosham village car park.

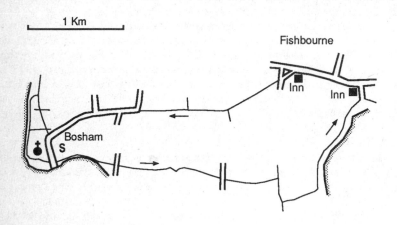

The first section of this walk cannot be undertaken at high tide for the right of way uses the foreshore. Instead, you should start at the church.

Walk back to the road, turn inland and go left into the lane beside the Millstream Hotel. Walk a few yards to a bend and there go ahead on an enclosed path at the rear of houses. Ignore the crossing paths, and on reaching the sea wall double back left along the shingle. Go inland through 'The Slip' to the churchyard. Keep the Anchor Bleu Inn for later and cross to a paved path that stays conveniently above the waterside road.

At the end of the creek, just before a brick pillar box, go left to a twitten beside the white bungalow. Enter fields, where, already, the influence of the sea has waned. Join a stony track, go right, around a cottage, and continue on field paths across the next lane. Go alongside a line of poplars, turn right, then left for the path around Fishbourne Creek. This path finds the sea wall and remains with it to reach a reed bed. Turn left at the mill pond for the village of Fishbourne.

On reaching the Bulls Head Inn, turn left along the still-busy coastal road. The Roman palace is signed $1/_2$ mile off route. Bear left beside the Black Boy Inn (with Charlie's Family Bar) and at the combined bend and junction, go ahead on what was a farm drive but is now only a path. Pass between a rubbish tip and nursery beds, continue along a line of poplars and then go on to a road.

It is now all tarmac back to the car, but there are a few thatched cottages to admire, and to keep your mind occupied the footway jinks from side to side. Acknowledge the Millstream and you are almost back. The car park is Pay and Display, so why not spend the rest of your parking time re-exploring the picturesque village of **Bosham** and contemplating the **age** of the inhabitants. Note especially the anti-flood measures adopted by the waterside properties.

POINTS OF INTEREST:
Bosham – When Chichester Harbour is mentioned, the image most likely to spring to mind is that of Bosham church as viewed from across the creek. An ancient settlement only recently addicted to pleasure boating, Bosham probably dates back to Roman times for neighbouring Fishbourne was a thriving port prior to the development of Chichester. Canute, whose daughter is buried at the church, came here early in the 11th century and from these shores made his impassioned plea against the incoming tide. King Harold Godwinson sailed from the port in 1064 to parley with William in Normandy. Both he and the church are depicted on the Bayeux Tapestry.

Age – How old is a 'Man of Bosham'? King James I granted all Bosham fishermen exemption from paying mooring charges. To preserve these rights, in 1938 Chichester Corporation promoted a bill through parliament. To qualify a 'Man' had to be born in the village prior to 1st December 1937 and to obtain his livelihood by harbour employment. Direct descendants also qualify provided they earn their crust in like manner.

REFRESHMENTS:
The Anchor Bleu Inn, Bosham.
There is a coffee shop in Bosham Walk.
The Bull's Head Inn, Fishbourne.
The Black Boy Inn, Fishbourne.

Maps: OS Sheets Landranger 197; Pathfinder 1266.

A visit to a forgotten village on a Roman road.

Start: At 870260, the NT car park on Woolbeding Common.

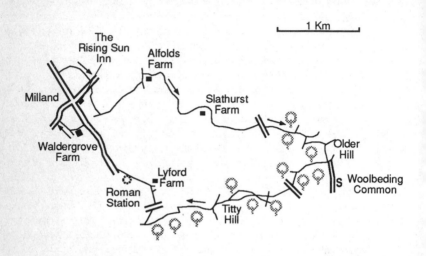

Leave the car park (which is situated on the single track road below Older Hill) and turn right along the road. After 220 yards, take the path on the left, dropping steeply through the Common's gorse and bracken. Go through trees to emerge by Bennetts Cottage, continuing downhill beside walls and hedges. Cross a track and re-enter woodland to reach a road near a sign proclaiming 'Redford'. Follow the path opposite (it can be boggy) and go diagonally across a clearing to enter more trees. Turn right and immediately left on to a path that rises to a junction of tracks and drives at Titty Hill. Take the grassy path opposite, going through chestnut trees along the lower slopes of the hill. Pass houses, then zig-zag left and right, walking below trees, then veering across grassland. Pass a clump of pines, right, and just before a cemetery, turn back right to go through them to a stile on to a lane. Turn right for 80 yards, then go left to Lyford Farm and follow the drive to a road. The embankments of a Roman posting station surrounding Westons Farm are seen to the left. Turn right along the road, passing a chapel, then leave the Roman road by turning left along the drive of Waldergrove Farm. Pass to the right of the buildings, then go half-right to a field corner and cross a footbridge to reach a road near a timber workshop. Turn right into **Milland**: the Rising Sun is beside the cross-roads.

Walk up the Liphook road and opposite a thatched cottage (unusual in these parts) take a path, right, which passes a barn and bears right to a road. Cross, go through fields, then bear left at a cottage along a path to Alfolds Farm. Walk around the farm buildings and houses then go along the modern drive. (This last section is currently unsigned). Turn right along Lambourne Lane and, after crossing a stream, start an almost imperceptible climb. At the end of the tarmac, turn left along the track to Slathurst Farm. Titty and Older Hills now begin to threaten to your right. Go around the farm on to a track that leads south, then east to meet a road near another 'Redford' sign. Cross diagonally right and climb a stile beside an old gate. Walk up to woodland, and up again through the trees. Near the top, turn right alongside a broken fence, then go back left up a sunken path that climb through bracken before sinking to rest beside Older Hill Kennels. Now turn right back to the start.

POINTS OF INTEREST:

Milland – This is an introverted village, rejected by Chichester, yet unable to co-habit easily with its nearer Hampshire neighbours. Persistent tales of a 'lost' Roman town in the district were given partial credence when, in 1949, the section of the Chichester to Silchester road, north of Iping, was confirmed from air photographs to pass through the village. The Westons Farm site, bisected by the modern road, has yet to be excavated. The date of the road is still uncertain, but coins dating from circa 70AD were discovered on the direct line of the road, suggesting it was in use by then. Another 'story' suggests Titty Hill as a lookout position protecting the posting station below.

REFRESHMENTS:
The Rising Sun, Milland.

Maps: OS Sheets Landranger 198; Pathfinder 1267 and 1246.
A walk through the grounds of this famous establishment.
Start: At 132288, Itchingfield Primary School.

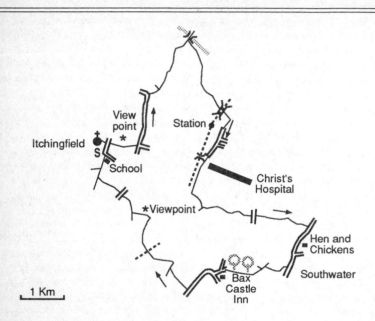

From the school, the **Church of St Nicholas** is clearly visible: it is reached through a short cul-de-sac. After your visit, retrace your steps and take the broad grassy track opposite the wisteria-covered cottage. In a few yards a vista presents itself: the Surrey Hills dominate the northern skyline, **Christ's Hospital** tower is prominent in front, while Horsham tries to hide behind the trees. Continue to reach a road and turn left. After about $^1/_2$ mile, at a sharp left-hand bend, follow the Downs Link signpost, then continue along a bridleway to reach a bridge over the infant River Arun. Take a path on the right which accompanies the river for a while, then enters woodland, crosses under the railway and arrives beside Christ's Hospital Station.

Walk past the modern houses, going along King Edward Road almost to the west gates of the school grounds. Another Downs Link sign now indicates a path to the right of the main entrance. An easy and peaceful walk through the school grounds follows, firstly beside the railway, then breaking left to follow bridleway signs through the well-maintained sports fields. Finally go along a drive (Road Closed) to reach a road. Cross and follow the bridleway opposite which gives softer walking to reach the Old Worthing Road at the edge of Southwater.

This village, thanks to its bypass, has become a typical urban sprawl of modern 'development'. Thankfully the walk avoids most of this: go past the Hen and Chickens, and opposite Coles Restaurant take a footpath, right, squeezed between houses. Go diagonally across the first field to a water tank and through a hedge to follow a path, via Courtland Wood, to the Bax Castle Inn. From the inn walk over the bridge and turn right. The second path on the right, besides Lawsons Farm, now crosses fields to join another path just south of the restored Little Stammerham Farm. Go past the farm and turn left, going around the training school building and continuing to a gated railway crossing. A farm track now climbs Sharpenhurst Hill. Although this track only reaches a height of 250 feet (75 metres), the view of the Downs from it is superb. Easily recognized are Amberley Mount, the dip of Washington Bostel, Chanctonbury, Truleigh – with its clutter – and Nyetimber. Magnificent.

Follow the track to a road and cross on to an enclosed path. On reaching the drive to Muntham House turn right for a five minute stroll back to the start.

POINTS OF INTEREST:
Church of St Nicholas – In the churchyard stands a tiny Priests House. It was probably used originally as a temporary lodging for a travelling priest from Sele Priory at Upper Beeding. The earliest part of this half-timbered building dates from the 15th century, the remainder having been built around 1600 when it was converted to an almshouse. From 1854 until the turn of the 20th century it was used as a vestry for the church.
Christ's Hospital – The conglomerate of red brick buildings of the hospital are more typical of a small town than those of a school. Designed by Sir Aston Webb, building started in 1892 and was completed in 1902 when the school moved from London. The school was founded in 1553 by Edward VI. Known as the Blue Coat School, a name derived from its unique uniform, the school became co-educational in 1985.

REFRESHMENTS:
The Hen and Chickens, Southwater.
The Bax Castle Inn, Two Mile Ash.

Walk 40   THE UPPER ROTHER VALLEY   6½m (10½km)

Maps: OS Sheets Landranger 197; Pathfinder 1266.

An easy walk through communities where time stands still.

Start: At 867218, a lay-by directly opposite the Bepton Road, on the A272, 1¼ miles west of Midhurst.

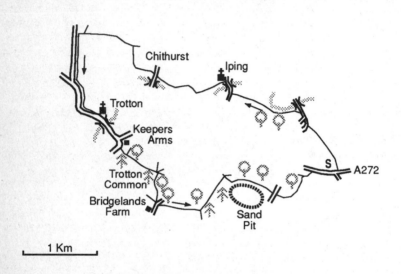

Take the footpath 50 yards east of the lay-by down to a footbridge amongst trees. Go over and climb to cross the polo fields of Great House Farm. Aim for a white building (if a match is in progress there is a waymarked alternative route), then walk along the front of the cottages and turn right at a road. At the next junction continue downhill, then immediately prior to a bridge go left on a bridleway beside the river. When this path climbs, the river loops away, but rejoins later. Walk beside a cottage and carefully down a cobbled slope to a lane. Do not take the path opposite: instead, turn right to cross Iping bridge. Enter the churchyard, and in the next field bear half-left to a shattered oak, continuing on a wide headland to a footbridge. The path beyond leads towards farm buildings, passing to the left of a red-tiled stone barn. At the farm follow the drive to a tree lined lane. Turn right into **Chithurst**, then left beside the church, along the drive of Chithurst Manor. Follow a path into fields, turning uphill. After passing through a belt of trees turn left along Brier Lane to a road. Turn left, climbing bracken covered steps to a roadside path that segregates you from the traffic. At the first house step down, with care, on to the busy A272 and continue past **Trotton Church** to the village's medieval bridge. Continue for 200 yards to a junction by the Keeper's Arms.

The return half of the walk traverses totally different countryside. Walk up the lane beside the inn and, after 150 yards, a sandy track on the left leads up to Trotton Common. At a junction of paths, on a pine covered knoll, break right, alongside trees, and descend off the sand to cross a road near Bridgelands Farm. About 50 yards past a metalled drive, turn left to walk with wooden power poles. Beside the drive entrance, on a road corner, cross a track into a stand of pines, then at the next crossing turn right on to a footpath that skirts the Minsted Sand Pit. Cross another road, and pass several up-market houses and cottages, beside the last of which (Quaggs Meadow) fork left to the common. Rejoin the A272 beside the house and sheds at Woolmers Bridge, and turn right with care for a final 300 yards back to the start.

POINTS OF INTEREST:

Chithurst – The village was once well known for its troupe of mummers, or in Sussex, tiptoers. The all male group performed their play at Christmas time in various local houses. A story of conflict, always with a happy ending, featured such bizarre characters as a Turkish knight, Father Christmas, the Devil, King or St George. The traditional script and score were never put to paper and were augmented each year with topical items. The players retained a permanent character for life and were only replaced in the event of death or serious illness.

Trotton church – The church contains a selection of wall paintings dating from the 14th century and two early monumental brasses, all celebrating the Camoys family. The earliest brass in the floor of the nave (protected by carpet) is of Margaret de Camoys who died around 1310. It is the earliest full length brass of a woman still in existence in England. The second brass, on a table tomb in the chancel, is of Thomas de Camoys, a soldier who distinguished himself at the Battle of Agincourt.

REFRESHMENTS:
The Keepers Arms, Trotton.
There are also many opportunities in nearby Midhurst.

Walk 41   HARROW HILL $6\frac{1}{2}$m ($10\frac{1}{2}$km)

Maps: OS Sheets Landranger 197 and 198; Pathfinder 1287 and 1306.

An easy downland walk to isolated farmsteads.

Start: At 087119, Chantry Post car park.

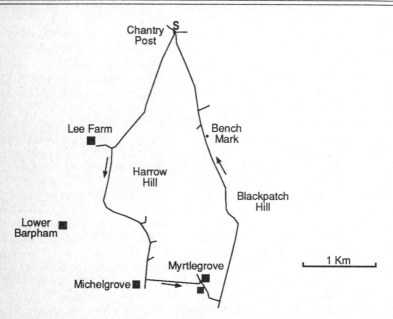

A bridleway, beside a wire fence, drops gently downhill (south-westwards) for over a mile to reach the drive of Lee Farm. The lower section of this path is over-shadowed by the pudding shaped hump of **Harrow Hill**. On reaching the drive double back through the adjacent gate and head for a distinct track heading over the shoulder of the hill. Across the valley, half hidden by trees, is the lonely farm of **Lower Barpham**.

The path is rather faint in the fields, as a guide, keep close to the power lines – these rejoin the farm drive at a sharp bend. Continue along the drive to **Michelgrove**, then turn left beside a high wall. The path now leads to the next farm at **Myrtlegrove**, more of a mini industrial estate than a traditional farm.

Where the access drive turns south, break left to rise beyond the barns and a small caravan site. Although continuing to gain height, the route keeps below the summit of Blackpatch, undulating across open downland. Look out for the stone tablet beside the path – an ancient OS bench mark still shows on its face. Where a bridleway leaves to the right, a signpost points into the field. Do not follow it: instead, continue along the field edge until you see the next direction sign, then make for it. In the last field, below the crest of the hill, you can practise your compass skills, a bearing of 340° takes you back to the car park.

POINTS OF INTEREST:

Harrow Hill – The hill is speckled with the craters of ancient flint mines: this is the site of a Neolithic hill fort. There is also evidence that at a later date the Romans took over the encampment. Many years ago a local downsman found half the base of a Samianware cup that had surfaced from a rabbit hole. He returned the following year and – yes – the obliging bunnies had excavated the remaining section!

Lower Barpham – This is the site of another Sussex 'lost village', the church having been pulled down in 1500. When viewed from Harrow Hill the earthworks of the early buildings show prominently in the field behind the farm.

Michelgrove – This, too, was once a larger place. It has lost its manor house, once sited behind the high wall, now demolished parts of the fabric still exist elsewhere. The staircase resides in Burton Park House, while the clock still governs the time of Steyning High Street.

Myrtlegrove – An interesting letterbox nestles in the wall of the farm office at Myrtlegrove. Well protected by numerous coats of paint it is one of the earliest types of Lamp Box. It probably dates from around 1910. Fifty years later there were over 21,000 of this type of box in use. This specimen still receives a daily collection.

REFRESHMENTS:

Nothing en route, but there are numerous possibilities in nearby Storrington.

Walk 42   **SELSFIELD AND GRAVETYE**   6¹/₂m (10¹/₂km)

Maps: OS Sheets Landranger 187; Pathfinder 1247.

In the wood and fields above West Hoathly.

Start: At 362350, the Forestry Commission car park at Vowels Wood.

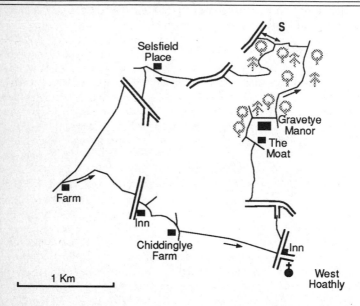

Go to the lower end of the car park, then turn right under the power lines and right again at a junction to climb up to the Drive Shaw viewpoint. Continue past the forestry board to the drive to Gravetye Manor. Turn right, and at the road go left for 300 yards. Turn right along the path beside the entrance to kennels going over the brow of a hill to Selsfield Place. Keep ahead on a wide grass path to a kissing gate. At the far edge of the Common break left to join a road between two drives. Turn right along the road, then left beside the wall of Wyndham Court. In the open field walk to a lone oak, then step right to maintain a south-westerly line. Now veer slightly right towards a farmhouse. Do not cross the stile: instead, return through the field following the line of power poles before dropping obliquely into a ghyll. Cross a footbridge, climb up an enclosed path and follow the Old House drive between two ornamental ponds to a road.

The White Hart Inn is a few yards to the right, but to continue the walk, go between two old stone gateposts and down to a bridge. Turn right among holly trees, circle below a red tiled house, re-enter trees and join a track up to a farm. Beside the house, fork left on a concrete drive, leaving it at a bend to coast through fields towards **West Hoathly** church. You arrive in the village opposite the Cat Inn. Turn left (or right from the inn), pass the village hall and, opposite the school, climb left along a short twitten to arrive at the edge of an estate. Leave the path and walk right between the houses to a road. Go left, then, at the end of the village, adjacent to the sign, go right to drop steeply into a valley to reach a swampy area, just before **the Moat**. Cross a stile and follow a semi-metalled drive as it begins its climb. Go above the **Manor House** and turn left at a junction. Slip right past Home Farm and, on entering a wood, take the left-hand track. Fork right into a stand of conifers and, beside a forestry board, double back left. Beyond the shallow steps, turn right, then keep close to the power lines to return to the start.

POINTS OF INTEREST:

West Hoathly – The centre of this hill top village is largely unscarred by modern development. The village was given to Anne of Cleeves by Henry VIII. Being adjacent to large tracts of woodland it was a popular haunt of smugglers, the Cat Inn being particularly favoured by them. Many buildings sport various types of adornment, some relevant, some commemorative, others just there. Even the bus shelter gets in on the act with a carved transom.

The Moat/Manor House – Gravetye was a manor from the 15th century – the yearly rent payable to King Henry VIII was one red rose. It became an iron foundry and the present house was built by the local iron master, Richard Infield, in 1597. The Moat is a 15th-century timber framed building built on an island in the original hammer pond. In the early years of this century the Manor was home to an aptly named horticultural journalist, William Gardener who at one time employed 18 workers in the estate gardens. On his death in 1935, at the age of 97, things quickly deteriorated. The house is now been resurrected as a luxury hotel and country club. The gardens, where there is a waymarked path, are open to the public on two days each week.

REFRESHMENTS:
The White Hart, on the route.
The Cat Inn, West Hoathly.

Walk 43   CUCKFIELD AND ANSTY   6¹/₂m (10¹/₂km)

Maps: OS Sheets Landranger 198; Pathfinder 1268.

A well wooded walk but with several pleasant open sections.

Start: At 304245, Broad Street Car Park Cuckfield.

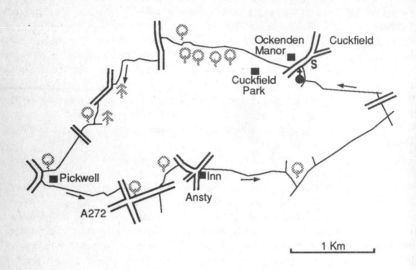

Descend the steps beside the toilets and turn left into the High Street. Wind round to the last house then go right into **Cuckfield Park**. The iron railings keep you away from the house, but both this and **Oakenden Manor**, to the right, are clearly visible. Cross a plank bridge then keep to the edge of woodland. At the corner of a high mesh fence veer half-left into the trees. Go over more planks and climb to a lane. Turn left along the lane, then right into the access track for Westup Farm. Keep ahead in the green lane: the path now turns left to a promontory of trees hiding a pond. Here, cross the field to a gap in the stand of conifers to reach a lane. Go left to a bridge and turn left, taking the right-hand path to climb a wooded slope. When you are rewarded with a view of the Downs, turn right on the crossing path. Go straight over at a lane, pass a small pond and then, prior to a collection of sheds, bear half-right before dipping down to reach another narrow road. Go left and left again into the drive to Pickwell.

Circle below the house, then follow the metalling for an enjoyable stroll through attractive mature gardens.

On reaching a road turn right for the A272. Turn left, with great care, along the main road, crossing to use the wider verge. About 50 yards beyond the **Ansty** village sign, re-cross, again with great care, to reach a narrow bridleway that runs between gardens, enters a copse and gets entangled with a wood yard. Go uphill for the village centre and inn. Take the unmade drive beside the inn and at the buildings go right into fields. Follow a track to a path junction and bear right, beside new plantings, to a pair of bridges. Turn left to follow an old tree-lined path that is an extension of Copyhold Lane. Beyond the first houses the track widens and becomes surfaced: detached houses and bungalows line the lane and an old sign points you left into a narrow enclosed path. Cross the **Cuckfield** by-pass with care, and bear left below the school to emerge into open fields. At a pond you join a track that rises slightly to go beside the cemetery. Enter the churchyard walk past the church and continue to the High Street.

POINTS OF INTEREST:

Cuckfield Park/Oakenden Manor – These are two examples of Sussex ironmasters houses. The Park was built in 1580 whilst the Manor, now a hotel, was purchased in 1608 by William Burrell who subsequently added to the 16th-century timber framed house.

Ansty – The name, pronounced with a long second syllable, derives from the Old English words for 'one path', ie. a narrow way, usually rising to a hill top settlement. The village still meets the criteria for the elevated situation. The signboard, now in need of a paint, shows a stag watching a horse and rider attempting to conquer a winding hilly path.

Cuckfield – This town or village, the choice is yours, developed on an old coaching route. It retains much of its old world charm thanks to a member of the Sergison family, owners of Cuckfield Park, who, in 1841, refused to allow the fledging railway to be built across their land. The line was diverted to the east, leading to the considerable increase of Haywards Heath. The Sergison name lives on in a hostelry in the latter town, named, it is said, in recognition of an annual gift of a buck for the local venison feast.

REFRESHMENTS:

The Ansty Cross, Ansty.
There are several possibilities in Cuckfield.

Walks 44 & 45   DITCHLING AND PYECOMBE   6½m (10½km) or 10m (16km)

Maps: OS Sheets Landranger 198; Pathfinder 1288.
A classic downland walk with an optional extension.
Start: At 303134, the Jack and Jill car park, Clayton.

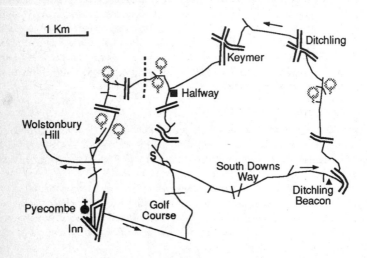

Walk back to Mill Lane and turn left. Follow the South Downs Way as it climbs steadily. At Keymer Post you cross the county border and continue in open downland. Continue to **Ditchling Beacon**: the trig. point at 813 feet is to the right. Go through the parking area and turn left along a road. After 130 yards take a bridleway, right. Turn left along a lane then right into Nye Lane. Go past a wood and a few yards beyond a culvert go right, off the main track. At the second stile veer half-left towards Ditchling church. Go over stiles to a drive to the village. Go right at the cross-roads, pass the shops and turn left into Boddington Lane. After a few yards go left to follow the line of a Roman road towards Keymer. Cross a footbridge and keep to the left hedge. Go left over a bridge and walk to a road. Turn right and, a few yards beyond the Greyhound, turn left. At the last house on the right walk into fields and go past a solo house (Halfway).

For the shorter walk, follow the house drive, left, cross a road and walk beside ponds, then round through houses to a lane. Turn left and at the bend, go right up a slope. Leave the waymarked path and trespass left on a track that climbs to the windmills and a car park.

The longer walk goes right on the track to another isolated house. Go left between woods to a railway bridge. At the road beyond, cross, right, and go ahead into trees. Turn left, and go past a farm, following its drive to a lane. Go left, then right on a bridleway that climbs over a shoulder of Wolstonbury Hill. At the top, turn right on a crossing path if you wish to reach the top. This adds $1^1/_2$ miles to the walk. Otherwise go ahead into **Pyecombe**. At the houses follow Church Lane to the inn. Keep behind the filling station, go left, then cross the Hassocks road and climb to a golf course. Cross a fairway and continue to a T-junction. Turn left to return to the start.

POINTS OF INTEREST:

Ditchling Beacon – There was a hill fort at the top but this has almost been demolished by farming and erosion. The name beacon derives from the hill's function as a warning station when the Armada threatened. The area was gifted to the nation by a gentleman in memory of his son who was killed in the Battle of Britain.

Pyecombe – The village was once the centre of a thriving downland industry, shepherd's hooks (more commonly called crooks) being made in the forge opposite the church. Their shape was unique and a perfection in design. So important was this instrument to the local economy that it features in the village sign and is adapted as a latch for the church's tapsell gate.

REFRESHMENTS:
The Greyhound, Keymer.
The Plough, Pyecombe.
There are also several possibilities in Ditchling.

Maps: OS Sheets Landranger 197; Pathfinder 1266.
A fine pair of Wealden walks.
Start: At 976278, the car park beside Ebernoe church.

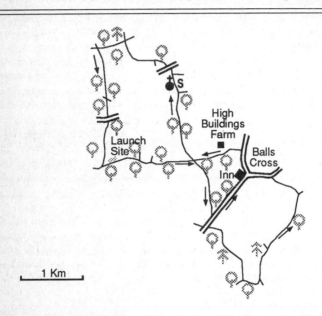

Return to the road, turn left for 40 yards, then right along a woodland path. Shortly
after passing a wooden gate, leave the main track by going left through the bracken.
Go ahead at a junction to reach a smaller gate, then drop to a footbridge. Cross the
centre of a field to a belt of trees and turn right to a metalled farm drive. Turn left: if
you look right between the belts of woodland you may spy a futuristic building, this is
the Midhurst air navigation beacon. Go left again on a little used bridleway. Head
south for over half a mile to reach a road. Keep to the right of the ornamental pond
and cross to the left-hand track. Go past the launch field for the British School of
Ballooning and follow the heavily used access track. Turn left to pass an artificial
fishing lake (not on the OS map) and continue past a farm to return to the trees of

Ebernoe Common. Ignore all side paths and shortly, after a narrower section, you will join a pair of grass-centred wheel tracks for a few yards.

Break right into a patch of bracken. The path leads to an area known as Pug's Bottom: you may forget the name but you will remember the path, glutinous Sussex mud! Lift yourself from the mire and on to a road. If you have had enough, or are on the shorter walk, go left along the road for 800 yards to the Stag Inn.

The longer route goes right. After 200 yards, take an unsignposted bridleway, left, which follows two inside edges of a wood before swinging left beside a stand of mature conifers, then right to pass under power cables. At the next junction turn left, and then left again for a short stretch of easier walking. Go under the power line again and continue, right, with more ruts and hoof prints. Ignore side paths, but if summer growth appears impenetrable follow the horses into a field. Return to the path line prior to crossing a stream. On meeting a farm drive, go left to a road. Turn left along the road to rejoin the shorter route at the Stag Inn, Balls Cross.

Follow the Northchapel road to the driveway for High Buildings Farm, on the left. Break left to miss the buildings, briefly joining the outward route before veering right towards Ebernoe woods. Go left into the trees. The path is easy to follow and signposted where needed: join a wider track and follow it back to **Ebernoe** and the start.

POINTS OF INTEREST:

Ebernoe Common – The Common, a Site of Special Scientific Interest, has probably been woodland since the Ice Age. For centuries it was used for woodland grazing, a fact confirmed by the abundance of large pollarded trees: since the cessation of grazing there has been an explosion of lower scrub. Later, the Common was put to industrial use. Furnace Pond suggests an iron foundry and a brick kiln, which operated until the 1930s, was supplied from the wood with clay and timber.

Ebernoe – Although only a hamlet, Ebernoe hosts a traditional English Fayre. The Horn Fair has continued on 25 July for over 500 years, apart from a gap during the Second World War when it was impossible to obtain a whole sheep for the roast. The ceremony starts early with the sheep being cooked slowly over an open fire throughout the day. Ebernoe play a local village at cricket and the horns of the roasted animal are presented to the batsmen making the highest score.

REFRESHMENTS:
The Stag Inn, Balls Cross.

Walk 48   CHARLWOOD   6³/₄m (11km)

Maps: OS Sheets Landranger 187; Pathfinder 1247 and 1227.
A countryside walk on the doorsteps of Gatwick and Crawley.
Start: At 251378, the Ifield Sports Field car park.

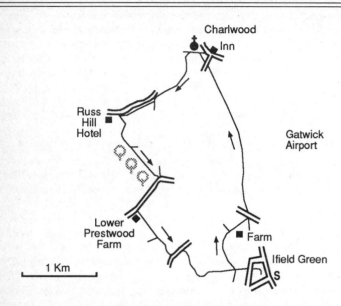

Walk into the sports field and at the club house turn across the grass to a gate. Opposite a path, to the right of an unmade drive, leads through brambles to a footbridge. Cross and walk ahead to a galvanised cattle drinking trough. Continue beside a hedge and at a house go through a gate and follow the track towards a farm. Pass between the sheds and follow the hotel drive to a road. Turn left for 30 yards, then go right on a path squeezed between fences and woodland. Go along the edge of the wood to arrive at an open field. Footprints may help a little but the field is largely trackless, so steer a little to the west of north, keeping to the left of the main strip of landing lights. Now aim for a fence corner, continuing with the fence to a tree stump. Break half-left back into the field, heading towards a farmhouse hiding behind trees. Go over a footbridge and follow the indentations in the next field to reach an enclosed path to a road. Go right to **Charlwood** village centre.

From the Rising Sun Inn, turn right, then cross into a narrow road leading to the church. Enter the churchyard and beyond the church entrance go left over a stile. (This is the Sussex Border Path, but you are in Surrey where it carries no waymarks). Cross to a hedge, then turn left to the first of a procession of stiles though a series of small fields. There is a **windmill** on your right. Keep to the side of the buildings of Windacre Farm: a stile gives access to a path parallel to the road but conveniently above it. At Russ Hill Hotel (a new name, so it may change again), turn left down a bridleway. This enters a wood, which is on the county boundary, then continues to a road. Go right for 600 yards, then turn left into the barns of Lower Prestwood Farm. Climb over the rise and on the same line drop down to a road at the entry to 'The Iffield Wood Conservation Project'. Go left, then right beside the cream timber clad cottage. Cross the infant River Mole, bear left along the bank and follow a well-trodden path to a footbridge crossed on the outward journey. Retrace your steps to the start.

POINTS OF INTEREST:

Windmill – The silent postmill below Windacre Farm is not a native of Charlwood, arriving from neighbouring Lowfield Heath. Its wind operation ceased in the 1880s, but a portable steam engine kept it grinding for a further 20 years. Two half-hearted attempts at restoration were made before, in 1986, a local trust was set up for its care. Unfortunately permission could not be obtained to restore on site – hence its removal to Charlwood.

Charlwood – In the 1970 local authority revisions, Charlwood, along with Gatwick Airport and Lowfield Heath, were transferred from Surrey to West Sussex. The local inhabitants protested so effectively that after a year in Sussex the boundary was re-drawn again and the village returned to Surrey. The village is currently threatened by the second Gatwick runway. In 1979 the British Airports Authority and the County Council signed a legally binding agreement preventing a further runway at the airport for 40 years, but the residents know that on the whim of any government this document could be overturned. The present mooted option for Runway 2 is to the east and north of the village. Over 550 homes would be destroyed or be uninhabitable. Charlwood would be squeezed out of existence.

REFRESHMENTS:
The Rising Sun Inn, Charlwood.

Walk 49   A LOOP ROUND LOXWOOD   7m (11km)

Maps: OS Sheets Landranger 186 and 187; Pathfinder 1246.

A walk near the Surrey border following an old canal.

Start: At 055318, the lay-by one mile east of Loxwood.

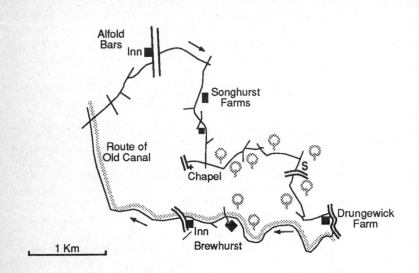

Cross the road, and take a path to the left of the white farmhouse. This enters woodland to join a wide track: be alert as the path suddenly turns right, joins another, then circles left around a pond before re-joining the track on its journey to Drungewick Farm. At a road, go right, downhill, then right again to cross a field towards a small wooden hut. Now veer right along the towpath of the old canal, following it for over 3 miles passing two restored features, an attractive bridge and Baldwin's Knob lock where there is a canal information board. At Brewhurst, leave the canal to view the old houses and water mill to the right. Return to the towpath: the canal bed is dry here, but beyond the lock water re-appears. A constructed path now reaches the **Onslow Arms**. Cross the road (the B2133) and continue to Devils Hole Bridge, from where the canal is derelict. The towpath is little better: pick your way through the mire for a mile, then, at a crossing path beside the remains of Barberry Bridge, go right on the

Sussex Border Path (SBP) through a belt of trees to a farm. Go along the farm drive and at the road turn left for the Sir Roger Tichbourne Inn.

Opposite the inn, the SBP follows Pig Bush Lane: the **county border** is just a stone's throw away here. At the top of a rise go right along the drive to the Songhurst Farms. A few yards before the 'New Farm' step left into a field and follow a headland path that skirts the barns before continuing southwards. Ignore the first side path but, at a crossing, turn right to the road beside **Cokeler's Chapel** (Emmanuel Fellowship). The unmarked graves of the Dependants are probably in the grass area to the rear of the building. Retrace your steps, then drop down to a marshy field and a footbridge. Beyond, follow a woodland path, leaving for a short field break, then re-entering. Turn left for 100 yards, then go right to emerge on to a track which shortly bears right to the car park.

POINTS OF INTEREST:

Onslow Arms – The inn was built at the same time as the canal and named after a local landowner and director of the company. The road that passes the inn became a turnpike in 1757. Toll collection ceased in 1876, but the toll cottage, next to the inn, remained until 1962 when it became a victim of road improvement.

County border – The closeness of the Surrey border proved an asset for one local policeman. Stationed in Loxwood when drunkenness was a common crime, his solution to the problem was simple – he collected the miscreants in a wheelbarrow, trundled them over the county line and deposited them in a Surrey hedge.

Cokeler's Chapel – In 1850 a London shoemaker arrived in Loxwood with his Society of Dependants. More usually known as 'Cokelers' this independent religious sect immediately found favour with the locals. The chapel in Spy Lane was established, and a series of co-operative shops were set up in this and other nearby villages. The shops were staffed by female adherents who always dressed in black. By 1885 there were over 2,000 followers, rejecting life's temptations of tobacco, alcohol etc. However, as marriage was frowned upon it is no surprise that the sect had almost disappeared by the early years of this century.

REFRESHMENTS:
The Onslow Arms, Loxwood.
Sir Roger Tichbourne, Alfold Bars.

Walk 50   **ARUN VALLEY WALK I**   7m (11km)
Maps: OS Sheets Landranger 197; Pathfinder 1287.
A longer walk along the Arun Valley.
Start: At 043186, Pulborough railway station.

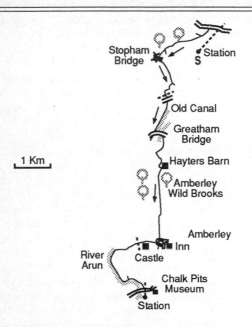

The Arun Valley Line has a regular hourly (two hourly on winter Sundays) train which can be used as a return on this linear walk.

Take the enclosed path between the station car park and the industrial estate to a road. Turn left and at the first bend, go left up the slope. A bridleway joins: continue to rise, passing a house and circling the tree-shrouded Park Mound. The path leaving left is a short cut to the river, but the walk continues ahead to the new bridge over the Arun. Cross to the White Hart Inn and **Old Stopham bridge**. Follow the access road to a stile on the right, go over and follow a path that uses a new footbridge to reach a water treatment works. Beside the last building, go right on a narrow concrete track, then turn beside a barn to reach the bed of the old Midhurst railway. Turn right for 150 yards, then go left over a railway bridge. Cross the A29, with care, and go half-right to a clump of trees near the gated entrance of the canal tunnel. The tunnel had no towpath; the barges were 'legged' through by the crew, lying on their backs and pushing against the tunnel roof with their feet. Follow the old towpath to a road and go left over Greatham Bridge. The path on the river bank soon reaches a farm track. Go through the farm, then bend right to the rejuvenated Hayters Barn. At signs indicating an area of open access, turn right on to the only right of way that crosses the **Amberley Wild Brooks**, finally rising up to the houses at Amberley.

The Black Horse Inn is to the left at the next junction, the church is on the western edge of the houses. After visiting, drop back to the water meadows beside the ruined walls of Amberley Castle. Only ever a castellated house this is now a luxury hotel. The track crosses the railway and reaches the river bank at the site of an old ferry. Turn left and follow the river downstream past the new South Downs Way bridge. The path veers to the rear of a caravan site and meets a road beside a railway bridge. The Bridge Inn is opposite and in summer there is a pleasant riverside tea room. Go under the railway bridge then turn right for the station and the entrance to the Chalk Pits Museum.

POINTS OF INTEREST:

Old Stopham bridge – This is considered to be one of the best medieval bridges remaining in Sussex. Seven arched and with refuges in the walls it was built in 1423 and carried the A283 traffic until the 1980s. The centre arch was raised in 1822 to allow masted vessels access to the upper river and canal. By the 1930s the increase in motor vehicles was causing damage to the bridge fabric and a system of alternate one-way traffic flow was introduced. The lights controlling the arrangement were the first to be introduced into rural Sussex.

Amberley Wild Brooks – The Wild Brooks is a patchwork of wetlands, marsh, open water and scrub. The central area was a raised peat bog, digging by the locals continuing until the Second World War. In winter the usual mode of transport was by boat but 'improved' drainage lowered the water table, many parts beginning to dry out. In 1978 a scheme to pump drain was vigorously opposed and defeated. Instead, the centuries old style of wetland management was reintroduced and the wild life is now improving with the winter wildfowl returning in greater numbers.

REFRESHMENTS:
The Black Horse, Amberley.
The Bridge Inn, Houghton.
Tea Rooms (summer only) Houghton.

Walk 51   NUTHURST   7m (11km)

Maps: OS Sheets Landranger 187; Pathfinder 1246 and 1267.
A visit to two estates which have known better times.
Start: The Carfax at Horsham.

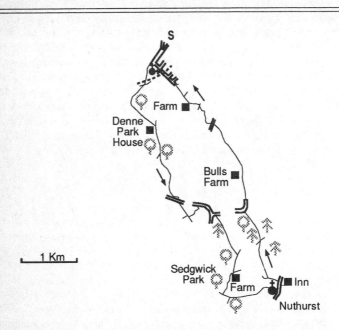

If you are parking in one of the town car parks, allow 4 hours for the walk.

Leave the Carfax at the south east corner, going around the Old Town Hall and walking along The Causeway, luckily unblighted by development, to the **parish church**. Go over the river bridge and continue beside the cricket field to reach a footbridge over the railway and the entry to **Denne Park**. Follow the path upward to the trees. On leaving the scrubby woodland, cross open parkland to a stile to the left of the buildings. Veer half-left across the next field to more trees and scrub. When clear of these, leave the main track to follow a footpath to the left. Alongside a newly planted area this path crosses to a pond, then edges beside young trees before crossing, right, to reach a road.

96

Turn left for 70 yards to reach a path, to the right, that aims for the far field corner and its adjacent barns. Here, turn left on a path that jinks back to the road. Turn right and follow the road to a T-junction. A few yards along Sedgewick Lane another path leads into the second park. Cross the abandoned air strip (no stiles) to a bunch of Leylandeii, then cross more parkland to reach the estate driveway.

Go downhill and join a track that passes Lower Sedgwick Farm. At the next path junction turn left for Nuthurst church. The Black Horse Inn is down to the left. Opposite the inn is the drive to Nuthurst Farm: take this, but just prior to the buildings break right to begin the only climb of the walk. In the re-planted wood, cross an access track then begin a gentle descent to the white gatehouse of the estate. Turn right along the road to reach the entrance of Sedgwick Home Farm. Just beyond, a path to the left first rounds the buildings of the ultra-smart Bulls Farm, then continues through fields to reach a road beside Amiesmill Bridge.

Cross the road and first field, then turn half-right to join a dampish farm track. Continue along the farm road back to Horsham. On reaching the houses walk the length of Chesworth Lane. Go under the railway and turn right into Denne Road. A final left into Normandy now returns you to the church and Carfax.

POINTS OF INTEREST:

Parish church – At the entrance to the churchyard, on the right, is a flat tomb askance to the other headstones. This is of a Muslim lady from the Middle East who married a local man and was accepted as English. Her husband subsequently deserted her. On her death she was buried across the east-west line to spare her the indignity of being thought a Christian.

Denne Park – Denne Park House is an 1870s rebuild of a 17th-century house, only a four storey tower of the earlier building remaining. Situated on a hill overlooking the town, there is evidence of early occupation, eg. the large ditch of an ancient fortification. The adjacent Picts Hill led some to think the name originated from Dan (Danes) Hill, but more likely is a derivation meaning woodland pasture, for in 1288 it was the recorded home of William Atte Denne.

REFRESHMENTS:

The Black Horse, Nuthurst.
There are also numerous possibilities in Horsham.

Walk 52   WEIR WOOD   7m (11km)

Maps: OS Sheets Landranger 187; Pathfinder 1247 and 1248.

A walk on the West Sussex side of the Weir Wood Reservoir.
Choose a dry day.

Start: At 409352, Weir Wood car park.

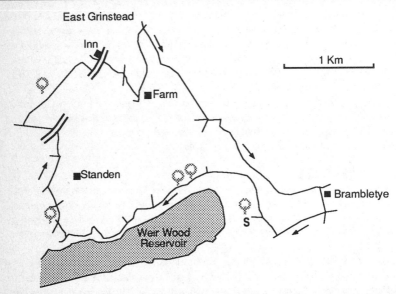

Return to the entry gate and take a path beside the brick wall that leads behind the water works and follows a wire mesh fence up to the corner of a wood. You must now follow an atrocious path for about a mile, a path squeezed between the reservoir fence and trees. The Sussex Border Path joins, then – bliss – the path crosses an open grassy field. Various paths climb left: ignore these, continuing along the morass until, at an information board, you enter an area with open access. Turn left just beyond a green roofed barn.

Ignore the stile on the right, it leads back to the barn, and go uphill to another board. Keep to the edge of the wood and carry on climbing to reach a wide fenced path. **Standen House** is to the right from here. Turn left into trees beside a drive, exiting through a parking area. Continue to a road. Go left for 50 yards into a sports field then follow a well-used path that drops, right, beside a wood. Go across two fields to arrive at the end of a cul-de-sac. Turn right along the humped private road, then left to the Dunnings Mill Inn.

From the inn cross into a recreation ground. The metalled path ends at the play area: follow the stream to a path junction and go half-right to farm buildings. Turn left along the farm drive which soon contains the spread of the East Grinstead housing. At a cross path beside the entrance to Great Harwood Barn, go right to a field oak, then continue to reach a couple of stiles. Cross a field to the first of a series of footbridges. At the next, where yellow waymarkers appear, bear left beside the stream. Where this executes a definitive loop, break across the field to the third, and more substantial, bridge. Cross, then, at the house, go right on a restricted path behind Horseshoe Farm. The path frees itself and rolls pleasantly towards **Brambletye**.

Skirt round the pond and barn construction then fork right in front of the house. Cross the river bridge and turn right into a field. The next concrete bridge is well hidden, but motorway type signs ensure that you continue in the right direction for the reservoir drive. Go right for 250 yards back to the entrance gate.

POINTS OF INTEREST:

Standen House – The house, now under the care of the National Trust, was a Victorian weekend retreat and, ultimately, retirement home of a London solicitor. One of the few houses designed by Philip Webb and built of local materials, it commands extensive views over the Sussex Weald, and more recently, Weir Wood. The interior furnishings are by Webbs friend, William Morris. Several examples of his distinctive wallpapers remain. The house is open during the summer months.

Brambletye – The ruined house at Brambletye was built in 1631 on the site of an earlier Saxon dwelling that was mentioned in Domesday. In 1683 the then owner, Sir James Richard, while riding in the forest was approached and warned that he was suspected of treason and that his house was about to be searched. Brambletye, left unoccupied and unclaimed gradually fell into ruin. The present house dates from 1919.

REFRESHMENTS:

The Dunnings Mill Inn, East Grinstead.

Walk 53   COWFOLD AND WINEHAM   7m (11km)

Maps: OS Sheets Landranger 198; Pathfinder 1268.

A level open walk exploring a selection from the myriad of paths below Cowfold.

Start: At 214225, Cowfold recreation ground car park.

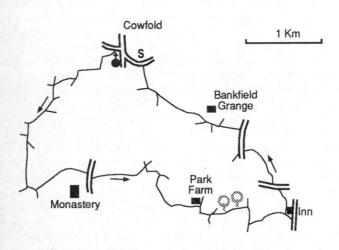

Go to the mini roundabout in **Cowfold** village centre, cross to St Peter's Cottage and follow the path through the churchyard. Turn left beside the school, then right to go around Gervaisse Cottage to a plank bridge. Cross half-left to join a crossing path. Turn left along the hedge, ignoring side paths and maintaining direction for about 1 mile. The elongated candelabra to the right is a relay station for a radio-phone operation. In the field before the low-slung farmhouse the line is to the right of the building, but it is easier to use the headland, joining the access track to the left of a house. Turn left, then left again at a junction to reach a road next to a Victorian letterbox now enclosed in a modern brick pillar.

Cross right to the drive for Gratwicke Farm, shortly veering to skirt the rear of the large house. Keep to the field edges before breaking to a tree-enclosed pond, here go right to a farm (Beware of the Bull). Keep to the edge of a field and, beyond the dung heap, steer away to cross a footbridge. Find a gap in bushes and a small gate, then continue to Park Farm. Step left for a better view of the ancient timber framed barn. Go right to enter a belt of trees. Zig-zag left, then right on to a grassy ride, keeping an eye open for deer. Take the left fork out of the trees and, at a white cottage, cross into the field. Follow the fence, right, to pass rearing pens. Before the next stile turn left for **Wineham Lane** and the Royal Oak. From the rear of the inn, edge beside a caravan park to a lane. Go left for 80 yards, then right to meander around a pond. Prior to another farm break left to a road. Turn right, then left into a metalled drive, the gate posts of which are emblazoned with numerous house nameplates. A few yards beyond the turning to Bankfield Grange, turn right across a field, a raised concrete section helping you to a footbridge. Keep to the left of the buildings and follow the access track away from the farm. Turn into the wood: the left-hand fork arrives at a paling fence protecting the houses. Follow this to a road and cross to regain the start.

POINTS OF INTEREST:

Cowfold – This is a village that tourists tend to ignore, but it has its quota of interesting buildings. St Peter's Cottage is a 15th-century Sussex timber frame complete with a Horsham slate roof. The old cottages around the church all face towards the place of worship, their backs are deemed good enough for the busy roads. The church contains one of the largest brasses in Sussex, sadly because of repeated vandalism it is rarely open for visitors.

The tall spire that dominates the countryside below Cowfold is not that of a church, but belongs to the Monastery of St Hugh. This secretive closed Carthusian order arrived unexpectedly from Paris over a century ago. Originally hidden in a wood the buildings are now more visible from the adjacent paths.

Wineham Lane – In January 1994 large parts of West Sussex disappeared under water. Wineham Lane was closed for three days, not through flooding but by the BBC. The Corporation had obtained permission from the county council for the closure to record an episode of the programme *999*, but omitted to inform the parish council or local residents. Takings at the Royal Oak were almost zero for potential customers faced a seven mile detour for their pint. Luckily no emergency services were needed that weekend.

REFRESHMENTS:

The Royal Oak, Wineham.
The Coach House, Cowfold.
St Peter's Cottage, Cowfold serves tea and coffee.

Walk 54   SMALL DOLE AND FIVE TOTTS   7m (11km)

Maps: OS Sheets Landranger 198; Pathfinder 1287 and 1288.
Starting with a riverside walk, then visiting the Downs.
Start: At 194105, the Upper Beeding Sports Centre car park.

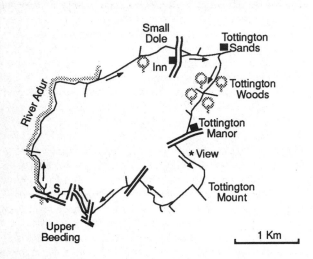

Leave the car park and walk back to the road. Turn right towards the river bridge. Do not go over the river: instead, turn right on the eastern bank. Pass a footbridge with an adjoining multi-directional signpost and continue along the river for another mile. As the Adur swings towards the outcropping Downs you collect a pair of wheel tracks. A glance to the right will reveal some of the local landmarks, Lancing College, Beeding Chimney and the Truleigh Hill aerials.

When the river resumes its northward journey, beyond the bushes, break right on a path which steers a north-easterly course. Cross a plank bridge and turn right along the edge of a wood before veering half-left through fields, to Small Dole.

You can continue by crossing into SandsLane, though a short detour to the right is needed to reach the Hare and Hounds. To continue, take the path opposite the inn and cross behind the football pitch to join Sands Lane. Go right to **Tottington Sands**

Farm. Before the buildings, turn right once again, going along an inter-farm track into Tottington Woods. These are attractive woods, heavily under-planted with hazel: notices invite you to enjoy the area, so it is a pity the owners see the need for a proliferation of 'Keep Out' signs.

Squeeze between the houses at Tottington Manor to reach a lane. Go right, then left to climb a steep, enclosed path. At a crossing fence rest and look behind you for a panoramic view over the Weald. Continue through open grassland almost to the summit of Tottington Mount. Follow the path as it bends towards the Channel. At the cross path, turn downhill, then break right on a slightly sunken path that winds down to a quarry. Now keep right around the lip before following the access drive to a road. Go left. Cross to the **filling station**, to the far side of which a road used as a public path rises over Windmill Hill. On reaching houses, continue through the trees and at a road go right, and immediately left, along a narrow lane. This 'street' takes you past ancient cottages inter-mixed with modern housing. Go straight over the next residential road into the **Upper Beeding** sports field: the start is to the left.

POINTS OF INTEREST:

Upper Beeding – People are sometimes confused by the siting and names of the two 'Beedings', Upper, only a few feet above sea level, and Lower, twelve miles inland and almost 300 feet higher. Their origins go back centuries to a form of chiefs and Indians. The more prosperous members of the tribe (the Uppers) were ideally situated, on the coast to become traders and merchants. The subordinates (the Lowers) were forced to scratch a living from the forest clearings.

Tottington Sands – The old chief 'Totta' certainly left his mark in the area. On this walk only the barn, a Youth Hostel, is missed. Tottington Sands is one of a series of farms blessed with the 'Sands' name. They extend eastwards in a line equidistant from the Downs and are all situated on a low ridge of sandy top soil.

Filling station – Goldring Barn, to the right of the filling station, was once a restaurant but has now been converted to a private residence. Legend says that it is the remains of a farm given by Oliver Cromwell, after the Civil War, to a certain Mr Goldyings 'for services rendered'.

REFRESHMENTS:
The Hare and Hounds Inn, Small Dole.

Walk 55   **AROUND KINGLEY VALE**   7¹/₄m (11¹/₂km)

Maps: OS Sheets Landranger 197; Pathfinder 1305 and 1286.

A hilly downward walk with two steep climbs. Not recommended on a sunny mid-summer afternoon.

Start: At 824088, the Nature Reserve car park 600 yards west of West Stoke.

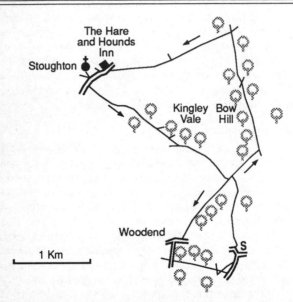

This walk does not enter the Nature Reserve but is intended as an introduction to the surrounding area. Why not return and explore Kingley Vale at your leisure?

From the car park take the adjacent footpath which gently climbs to the **Reserve** entrance. Do not enter: instead, turn right on a bridleway, then left at the next crossing to enter the edge of the Reserve below Bow Hill. The Trundle with its radio masts is prominent to the east across the Lavant valley. The chalk track steepens through scrubland: ignore the crossing path and go downhill, out of the trees, to reach a junction of paths. Turn left, and in a few yards the village of **Stoughton** becomes visible, snuggling in the valley below. This area contains many remains of neolithic tumuli and barrows, the majority covered by scrub and undergrowth. However, by looking back when descending, the hump of a long barrow can be recognized on the hill top. On gaining the road turn left for the Hare and Hounds Inn.

From the inn continue along the road to reach the miniscule village green. A path from here leads to the Saxon church, which is well worth a short visit. Return to the green then walk a few more yards to gain the bridleway beside the Tythe Barn House. This path commences its upward climb reasonably, but soon develops into a 'pipe opener' of a pull. On reaching the summit walk alongside woodland, then descend into a stand of yew trees. After collecting another path from the right, drop down beside the edge of the Reserve. The main section of the yew forest is to your left but hidden by scrub: after 100 yards, before the entry gate (and your outward journey), turn right on to a fenced, then enclosed, path to a road. Turn right, then left into Woodend. After 300 yards turn left again on to a pleasant, level woodland walk. Immediately after a crossing a bridleway turn half-left on to a footpath and follow it to the road beside the Old Rectory grounds. Turn left to reach a T-junction and, just beyond, the starting car park.

POINTS OF INTEREST:

Reserve – The English Nature Reserve at Kingley Vale is situated in and around a south facing coombe of the South Downs a few miles to the north-west of Chichester. Its yew forest, with many of its trees up to 500 years old, is considered to be among the best in Europe. Beside scrub and mixed woodland the reserve also contains areas of sheep-grazed chalk grassland. A way-marked nature trail will guide you around.

Stoughton – The village was recorded in the Doomsday Book as a Saxon manor. Probably the most famous of its sons was one George Brown, a cricketing colossus of early English fast bowling. Born in the late 1700s he could hurl a ball over 130 yards. In one match he bowled continuously for four and a half hours delivering 230 balls at a cost of 8 runs. So fiery was his bowling that the wicket-keeper used straw around his body as added protection. On one occasion at Lords, the longstop tried to restrain the missile by the use of a coat. The ball tore right through and killed a dog that 'just happened to be passing'.

REFRESHMENTS:

The Hare and Hounds Inn, Stoughton.

Walk 56   **KIRDFORD**   7^1/$_2$m (12km)
Maps: OS Sheets Landranger 186; Pathfinder 1246 and 1267.
A walk across Sussex clay with plenty of trees.
Start: At 041304, beside the pond at the junction of the Haslemere
road and the B2133.

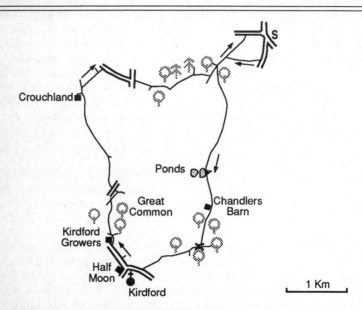

Cross the road and walk down Skiff Lane (signposted Kirdford). Turn right into the
drive of Beldhamland Farm and continue through fields to a wood. Enter and turn left
immediately on to a bridleway. At a junction of paths turn half-left beside a drive into
an overgrown area. Keep the barbed wire fence closely left and soon join a definite
path through trees. Follow this south, crossing a farm drive en route. A bridleway
joins from the right beside ornamental ponds: continue on a wide ride beside a line of
poplars to Chandlers Barn. Enter woodland behind the barn and in the second wood
bear right on a wide track crossing an ivy-covered bridge. Leave the bridleway beside
a pair of cottages, taking the footpath on the right around the edge of Barkfield Estate
to a road. Turn right to **Kirdford** and the Half Moon Inn, opposite the church. The
wall plaque is beside the bend before the road junction.

Follow the Petworth road and turn into Hetrons Close. The path beside No. 1 leads around the austere buildings of **Kirdford Growers** before turning away to cross the local football pitch. Enter the trees of Great Common, keeping ahead on the main path and cross a drive and a footbridge. Go over a second bridge and turn sharp left along a field edge. Go through a gate beside the white farmhouse to a road. Cross and follow the RUPP (road used as a public path – recognized in West Sussex by the absence of lettering on the signpost arms) northwards through trees and fields to reach Crouchland. Join a concrete drive and follow it to a road. Turn right and at the T-junction go ahead through wooden gates. The bridleway beyond leads between a golf course and orchards before entering Wephurst Wood. On exiting the trees turn left along the woodland edge before re-entering on a wide Forestry Commission track. Do not take the path to the left: instead, cross an open field and bear left to a path junction reached on the outward journey. Retrace your steps along the bridleway, but do not follow the footpath back to Skiff Lane: instead, continue ahead to reach the Haslemere road beside sports fields. Turn right along the road back to the start.

POINTS OF INTEREST:

Kirdford – The village sign at the road junction has a precis of local history on its base. The sign itself contains portions of locally produced glass. From 1300 to 1600 the primary local industry was glass making, because of ample supplies of timber for fuel and the right type of sand. Its demise was ensured by an Act of Parliament in 1615 forbidding the use of timber as a fuel for glass making. On the wall of the vicarage is a **plaque** advising of 'The Degredation of Drunkenness'. The plaque offers both medical and moral views, but despite it the village still retains two inns.

Kirdford Growers – This is the oldest apple co-operative in the country. In 1925 five local farms formed a loose association, more joined and in 1928 the Kirdford Fruit Growers Association was formed. At one time it boasted of having 17 local members but with the contraction of fruit farming in the area the number has reduced and 'foreign' apples from the south now find their way through the grading and packing sheds.

REFRESHMENTS:
The Half Moon, Kirdford.

Walk 57   THE CHICHESTER CANAL   7¹/₂m (12km)

Maps: OS Sheets Landranger 197; Pathfinder 1305.
Following the canal from the City to the sea.
Start: The market cross in the centre of Chichester.

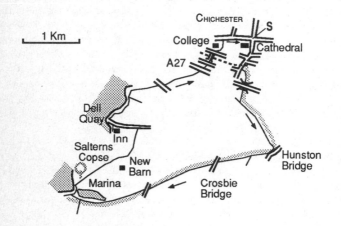

Walk down South Street, go over a level crossing and turn left into Canal Wharf on a footpath signposted to the rear of the Richmond Arms. On a lawn beside the **canal** is the first of the information boards passed along the towpath. Follow the canal out of the basin on a wide path: once under the road bridge the hassle of the city is left behind in favour of a more pleasant environment. The canal passes through a wide cutting, then moves into open fields before arriving at Hunston Bridge. Cross to the road, pass in front of Canal Cottage and rejoin the towpath as the waterway changes direction. The next walk section is particularly restful, the peace only broken by the snores of dozing fishermen. Seats are provided at regular intervals for walkers who wish to join them. The concrete abutment on the far bank is the only remains of a swing bridge that carried the Selsey Tramway across the canal, the footpath to the left using the track bed. Beyond Crosbie Bridge the water is largely reed covered. At the next, busier, road, cross on to a wide grassy path that merges with the drive to the yacht marina. At the information point keep to the left of the boats, which now includes a few houseboats. Pass 'The Spinnaker' (sailors only) and beside a long low shed turn right to cross over the lock gates serving the marina.

Cross a parking space and enter Salterns Copse. Beyond the trees the green roof of Chichester Cathedral is visible. Turn left at a new barn, going along a drive to reach a road. Turn left for **Dell Quay**: it is time to polish up your nautical memories if you wish to order at the Crown and Anchor. Walk down to the end of a flint wall, from where the path leads between boat yards into open fields. The first footpath to the right leads only to the church and houses at Apuldram: continue, but beside the second 'squeezer' stile leave the water's edge and bear right across a field to a stile adjacent to a prominent road sign. Cross the road and follow the indistinct path opposite as it wanders through meadows beside the River Lavant. (As a general direction, aim just to the right of the Cathedral). In the field before the A27 keep to the headland almost to the road. Cross the dual carriageway with great care, and take a miserable path through an industrial area to reach a long footbridge over the railway. A more amenable path beyond the ring road meets up with a cycleway to cross in front of college buildings. At Westgate, turn right for the Cathedral and Market Cross.

POINTS OF INTEREST:

Chichester Canal – The canal was authorised in 1819 as an arm of the longer Portsmouth and Arundel (P & A) waterway. The Chichester section was built to ship canal standard and could accept barges up to 100 tons. The P & A was only for use by smaller craft and closed in 1855. The Chichester carried its last commercial cargo in 1906 and was abandoned by its then owners, the City Council, in 1928. The whole (4 miles) length was purchased in 1957 by West Sussex County Council. There is an ongoing restoration programme.

Dell Quay – This was the Roman port for Chichester and remained a port until 1822 when the canal opened. Poor overland access to the city was the reason given for the canal construction. Dell Quay sent two ships to battle against the Spanish Armada, this action earning it special harbour rights from Queen Elizabeth I.

REFRESHMENTS:

Chichester – Many, from McDonalds to the Five Star.
The Crown and Anchor, Dell Quay.

Walk 58　　　　　BLACKDOWN　　　　7$\frac{1}{2}$m (12km)

Maps: OS Sheets Landranger 186; Pathfinder 1245 and 1266.
A wooded walk to the highest point in Sussex.
Start: At 890309, the National Trust car park at the southern end
of Marley Common.

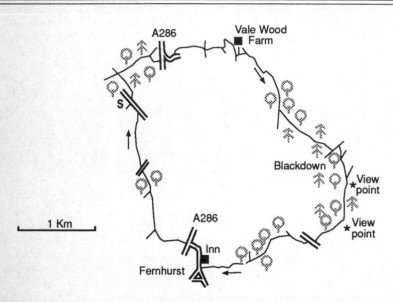

Cross the single track road to a yellow arrowed path, ignoring blue waymarkers but
turning left on to a wider track. Go over a drive to meet the Sussex Border Path
(SBP). Turn right and follow the Path. At first it passes through mixed woodland, but
then falls steeply to houses and the A286. Cross, with care, into Fernden Lane. Go
around a bend to where the SBP breaks left between the rear gardens of houses. A
brick wall appears to block your way: pass through the gateless arch, then turn left
into a swampy area and follow a narrow path to the entrance for Vale Wood Farmhouse.
Follow the drive and beyond the house turn into another National Trust area. At the
iron gate turn uphill on a bridleway to rejoin the SBP at a field corner. Cross another
field, then enter woodland and climb steadily to the top of **Blackdown**. The area is criss-
crossed with paths, several of which will take you to the top, but our route only touches

the 900 foot contour. Where a bridleway leaves to the right, follow the SBP leftwards, but soon turn right between wooden barriers (for horses) on to the narrow Pen-y-bos track. At the next barrier, continue straight ahead on a bridleway to meet another at a contrived, but limited, viewpoint. The right-hand path takes you to the southern section of the hill known as **the Temple of the Winds** where there is another viewpoint and a rustic seat. Descend now, and after a steep rough gully cross a road into the drive of 'Reeth'. The glasshouses below belong to the Zeneca agricultural research station. Turn left beside the house and, at a dark barn, keep right to continue through the trees all the way to the Red Lion at **Fernhurst**. From the inn take the road going uphill, along the eastern fringes of the village, and at the main road cross to reach a path behind houses. Go over a footbridge and up steps, then turn right along a tarmac road (used as a public path – RUPP) that loses its surface when it enters chestnut coppices. Climb steeply to a road, cross and continue uphill to reach houses. Now follow the RUPP as it levels beside a conifer nursery, and when a road is reached turn left for the car park.

POINTS OF INTEREST:

Blackdown – At 917 feet this is the highest hill in Sussex, its name deriving from the sombre appearance of its pine clad upper slopes. It is crossed by many ancient tracks, Pen-y-bos dating back to Celtic times. Because it was half-way between the coast and London, the Down was the reputed haunt of smugglers. According to local lore there is a yet to be discovered cave where contraband was stored prior to distribution.

The Temple of the Winds – Alfred, Lord Tennyson built Aldworth House on Blackdown's lower slopes and lived there for 24 years. He also erected a summerhouse on the adjacent top and suffixed its name of 'The Temple' with 'of the Four Winds' in recognition of its susceptibility to continuous breezes.

Fernhurst – The village was, for 200 years, one of the primary centres of the Wealden iron industry. Local names, eg. Minepit Copse, Ironhill Common and Furnace Wood all indicates sites of activity. The export of the finished product ravaged the inadequate 'roads', and it was therefore mainly due to this destructive commerce that, in 1749, the first exclusive Sussex Turnpike Trust was set up. Its aim was 'to repair the road from Hindhead Heath through Fernhurst Lane to Midhurst and Chichester'.

REFRESHMENTS:
The Red Lion, Fernhurst.

Walk 59　　　**ARUNDEL PARK**　　　7¹/₂m (12km)

Maps: OS Sheets Landranger 197; Pathfinder 1306 and 1287.
A fine parkland and river walk.
Start: At 020070, the river bridge, Arundel.

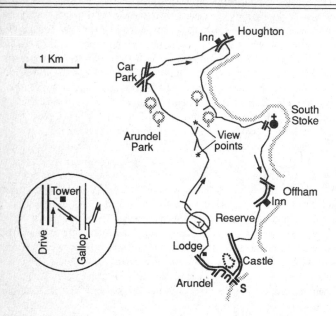

Walk up the High Street and follow the castle wall around to enter the Park at the lodge. The Park is open daily (except 24 March) and the public has free access over its paths. Dogs are not allowed. From the gate go along the drive to the **tower**, then half-right across the grass and training gallop to a track that falls gently above the head of Swanbourne Lake. Dip down to a crossing, then walk ahead on a track that climbs the hill below the public footpath. Before a wood, turn left on a track to a viewpoint of the castle and the river towards Littlehampton. The footpath rejoins, but leaves again at a second viewpoint, here of the river and Downs and inland to the Weald. Bear left over the grass to join a track along the hillside to Whiteways Lodge. The exit from the park is to the right of the gatehouse. Cross the roundabout to the car park and snack bar.

Walk north, beside the road, to the end of the scrub, then cross on to a bridleway which immediately begins to descend into the valley. Pass in front of a house and emerge at the **George and Dragon Inn**, Houghton. Continue to a cross-roads. Turn right into South Lane. At its end a path edges towards the river beneath a steep clematis covered bank. After a small grassy area, protected by sheer chalk cliffs, the path is squeezed between the estate wall and the river. Eventually follow the wall inland. Do not enter the estate: instead, continue into an area of box trees and roller-coaster along to the farm at South Stoke. Keep to the right of the buildings and take the path above the church. Pass the quaintly named 'Foxes Oven' to join a road. Turn left, then right at the T-junction to go along a sunken lane. Pass the Black Rabbit Inn to rejoin the river as it flows behind the wildfowl reserve. Follow the reserve fence round to a road. Turn left for a pleasant amble along Mill Road back to town.

POINTS OF INTEREST:

Tower – The Hiorne tower was designed by the architect Francis Hiorne and built in 1797 as a 'sampler' for a contract he was hoping to win – the rebuilding of the castle. However he was unlucky for he died two years later. Although it has habitable rooms it is no longer used as a residence. The stone urn positioned in front of the tower was taken from the museum at Sebastapol after the 1855 siege. It is unclear as to why it was presented to the Duke of Norfolk.

George and Dragon Inn – The timber framed inn once played host to a royal visitor. King Charles II, after his defeat at the Battle of Worcester arrived with two companions around midday on 14 October 1657. Nearby Arundel, was a Cromwellian stronghold, its troops scouring the countryside for the fugitive. Charles, playing safe, declined to dismount and took his refreshments en saddle. He arrived in Brighton safely and at midnight sailed for France.

REFRESHMENTS:
Whiteways Lodge Snack Bar.
The George and Dragon Inn, Houghton.
The Black Rabbit, Offham

Walk 60   **POLING**   7¹/₂m (12km)

Maps: OS Sheets Landranger 197 and 198; Pathfinder 1306.
A linear walk in the levels behind the coastal strip.
Start: At 024064, Arundel Station.

For the return journey there is an hourly train service back to Arundel. Change at
Ford. On winter Sundays this frequency reduces to every two hours.

From the station return to the road, cross the bridge and take the path on the right
through fields, passing just to the right of farm buildings. Continue beside a wire
fence before bearing right to a stile. A slightly raised bank leads to a footbridge and
an enclosed path alongside the **Knucker Hole**, now protected by the fence and thicket
of willows. At the front of the church go ahead towards the farm, turning left at a
warning notice. Keep close to the garden fences, then cross to a roadside stile beside
the caravan park. Turn right and, after 80 yards, cross to a path on the left. This turns
half-left through paddocks to rejoin the road for a few yards. Take a bridleway on the
right and follow it to **Poling**. There a path is signed to the church. Go over a stile at the
eastern end of the churchyard to return to the path, which ends at a gate. Keep right in

the field beyond and cross a footbridge. Take a flight of steps into the next field and aim towards the house with the prominent chimney, going midway between two barns. Go straight ahead along a road, ignoring a path to the left, to reach the A280 junction. Turn left for the Angmering centre and the Lamb Inn.

Go along the B2225 (Ferring) and, at the right bend, turn into the No Through Road. Pass the Spotted Cow, turn right at the junction for 50 yards, then go left to climb Highdown Hill. As you rise into scrub the path surface deteriorates. A footpath climbs to the left: after 20 yards, at the National Trust sign, go uphill on a bridleway. to reach open downland. Now follow the clear path up to the earthworks. Although only at 265 feet, the hill offers a fine view over the channel. From the top drop down to the left of a reservoir fence, then follow a track to the dual carriageway (A259). Cross, with care, into Ferring Lane. At a bend a twitten heads towards the railway: turn left on the lineside path to reach Goring Station.

POINTS OF INTEREST:

Knucker Hole – The pond is named from the old English word 'nucar' meaning a sea monster. Legend has this pond to be bottomless for it never freezes in winter nor evaporates to any degree in summer. It was home to a dragon who seized livestock or herders, dragging them on to the adjoining marshes for a leisurely meal. The monster was finally slain by either a knight in shining armour who claimed the local princess for his bride or a local lad who asked nothing for his efforts. Local stories offer both versions.

Poling – This is one of the smallest parishes in the county with an electoral register of around 150 souls. In World War II the population doubled with the installation of a defence radar station. The site was temporarily knocked out by a German air attack in August 1940 but not finally closed until 1955. A Royal Air Force standard was presented to the village in recognition of its close association with the service. Poling church contains the only surviving poor box in Sussex. Iron bound, it is dated 1285. Note the faux-pas in the spelling on the tablet above.

REFRESHMENTS:

The Lamb Inn, Angmering.

Walk 61   BALCOMBE AND STAPLEFIELD   7½m (12km)

Maps: OS Sheets Landranger 187; Pathfinder 1247 and 1268.

A walk over Balcombe ridges to the Upper Ouse vale.

Start: At 307301, Balcombe railway station.

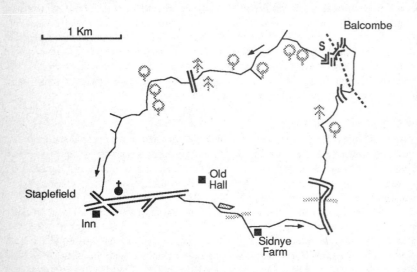

A charge is made for parking at the station, free parking is available beside the church, ½ mile to the north.

At the entrance to the car park a path steps down to a bend on a narrow lane. Go over a stile to the right of the house and climb up the field beyond. Follow the top edge of a wood to a farm drive. Fork left for the farm, leaving on a track that goes around to a narrow belt of woodland. Go right, dip to a plank bridge guarded by steps and a handrail and then climb through pines to a lane. Opposite is the drive for Brantridge School. Keep to the left of the main building, but before the farm slip into a field. Drop down into a wooded ghyll and, immediately after crossing the stream, climb to the edge of the trees. Turn left on the remains of an old track, skirt round the next set of buildings and turn left along a concrete drive. Continue on this grass-centred drive to Staplefield. On reaching the Green, cross to the **Victory Inn**.

Now walk towards the church and enter Brantridge Lane. Pass both the **church** and school and keep left at the road junction. Walk beside the entrance to Tye's Place and turn into the drive to reach three cottages. Bisect the buildings and break right on a garden path. Cross a stile and go left along a field edge. Old Hall, with its Kew-like conservatory keeps an eye on you. Listen to the honking of the waterfowl as you walk between the tree-enclosed water and the infant River Ouse. Cross a footbridge and aim for the chimney pots of Sidnye farmhouse. Go left through the buildings and follow their access track to a lane.

Turn left to a bridge. Go over a stile to the left, or use the gap, then steer towards the house on the skyline. Re-cross the lane and, still rising, go to the right of the house (and garden?). At the top of the slope the half-hidden houses of Balcome beckon, but you must drop down again into the trees. Continue the roller-coaster to the left of a derelict pond to reach a road. Cross and go left to reach a metalled drive on the right. Walk in the front of Kemps House, then edge right and go over a foot crossing of the railway.

Climb up the side of the cutting and follow the edge of the wood to houses. Turn left along the residential road: a short path leads left to a telephone box on the main road. One entrance to the station lies opposite.

POINTS OF INTEREST:

The Victory Inn – The inn, with its multitude of menu boards, boasts that on offer each day are a total of 365 different main courses, one for every day of the year. Originally a grocery shop, the proprietor wanted to convert part into an inn but his first application was unsuccessful. After a suitable period of time had elapsed he tried again and a licence was granted. On leaving the quarter sessions, mine host debated with the supporting brewery director the name of the future inn. 'Today' replied the brewer 'you have a victory, why not call it that!'

Church – Staplefield parish church is relatively modern, a typical early Victorian Anglican place of worship. In 1877 the vicar, concerned that the timekeeping of pupils at the adjacent school was not up to standard, had a clock installed in the church tower. He was not amused to find a few days later that the face being used as a target for the pupils' catapults.

REFRESHMENTS:
The Victory Inn, Staplefield.

Walk 62   **HORSTED KEYNES AND ARDINGLY**   7^1/$_2$m (12km)
Maps: OS Sheets Landranger 198; Pathfinder 1268.
Up and down and around the Bluebell Railway.
Start: At 384282, the car park behind the British Legion Hall,
Horsted Keynes.

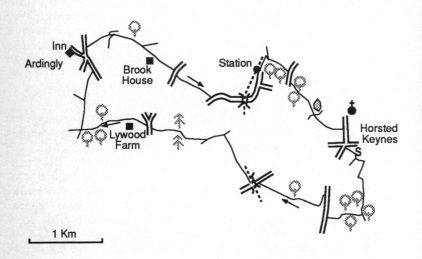

Go down the unmade road beside the Hall, continuing along Wyetts Lane and following
the Sussex Border Path signs into a wood. Turn right on a track, clear the trees and go
across a field towards a bungalow. Go right along a road, and at the top of a rise
double back left to the rear of Keysfold Hall. Go down into a belt of trees and, in the
next field, aim to the right-hand hillside farm. Go under the railway bridge and
immediately turn right along a farm road. Miss the buildings and, at a junction, go left
to a footbridge and stile. Take the path that rises half-right and, in the second field,
veer slightly left to follow the field edge round to a wide ride through a conifer
plantation. Cross the road to Lyewood farm drive. Go past the barns and down to a
bridge, continuing through scrub. In a field beyond, go half-right to join a path that

rises towards the Ardingly. Do not go left on the track: instead, continue through fields to a road. Turn left for the village centre. The Oak Inn is along Street Lane.

Return to the cross-roads and turn left. An alley opposite the Post Office enters fields. Descend steeply, pass an isolated house and follow a fence to a bridge. Climb a slope, go to the rear of the cricket pavilion and edge round the gardens of Brook House. Where the path bends right towards a drive, go ahead beside a fence. Go right along a road for 30 yards, then left on a path which enters a garden then crosses an open field by black and white posts. At the next road turn left, going under a **Bluebell** arch and then turn left to Horsted Keynes station. Go through the car park and turn right on a path along the edge of Leamland Wood. At a road, go right for 80 yards, then cross a stile, left, into woodland. Keep right of a pond and go straight over a cross path. Now bear left and up to a lane. Turn left for the **church** or right to regain the start.

POINTS OF INTEREST:

Bluebell – The Bluebell Line is part of the original East Grinstead to Lewes railway opened by the LBSCR in 1882 and known as the Sheffield Park Line. It was first closed in May 1955, but local opposition discovered that British Rail had contravened the original act and forced a re-opening for three years until a new act was formulated and passed. The section between Sheffield Park, where the locomotives are housed, and Horsted Keynes which looks after the passenger and goods vehicles, was opened in 1960 as the Bluebell Line. In 1980 a share floatation to raise funds for future expansion brought in £38,000. Trains now travel to New Coombe Bridge, north of West Hoathly.

Horsted Keynes Church – Inside is a 27 inch long monument to a 13th-century knight. It is believed to be a heart burial, probably that of a member of the Cahainge family from whom the village name has evolved. When a crusader knight was killed abroad his body was buried in foreign fields, but his heart was returned to England. Another unusual tablet in the chancel is to Henry Piggott who apparently died before he was born, December 30th to March 7th 1715. It is not an error – at that time the Julian calendar was till in operation, New Year's Day being 25th March. The unlucky child therefore lived for only nine weeks.

REFRESHMENTS:

The Oak Inn, Street Lane, Ardingly.

Walk 63   **HENFIELD AND MOCK BRIDGE**   7¹/₂m (12km)
Maps: OS Sheets Landranger 198; Pathfinder 1288.
A visit the head of the Adur Navigation.
Start: At 215159, Henfield High Street. There are car parks on
both sides of the road.

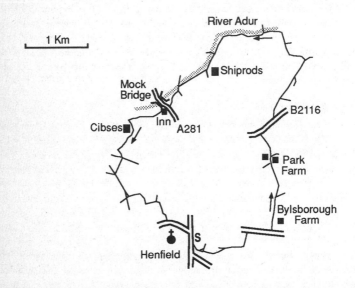

From the car park of your choice return to the High Street and walk south (slightly uphill). Turn into the alley beside the George, go through the parking area and garden, and into a twitten. Go right at the squeezer, then left along the commonside road. Go half-left beside a gravelled drive and keep ahead at a junction. Drop off the ridge to pass between orchards then turn right along a single track lane. At the top of the rise go into the drive to Bylsborough Farm and beside the thatched house go temporarily into fields. Now rejoin the metalling for an easy stroll through Park Farm and on to the B2116. Turn right, then left off the road at a set of barns on a sharp bend. Continue on a typical tree-lined Sussex bridleway, but shortly after the path opens, leave it by breaking left into fields. Ford a stream, climb to circle a farm, then keep ahead to reach the River Adur.

Keep to the river bank, turning away at the weir towards Shiprods. In front of the house there is a path junction: go right, with a hedge on your left. At the second part of the staggered crosspath follow the upper river bank to a stile, then cross two fields to reach the A281. **Mock Bridge** is a few yards to the right. Cross, with care, to the Bull Inn. From the inn, go immediately into fields, rounding the farm and barn conversion. Keep ahead, then bend left to pass in front of Cibses. Now walk towards the Downs, crossing a substantial bridge over a relatively small stream. Follow the access track from the next house up to the Downs Link trail. Turn left and, at the first opportunity, go left on a crossing path that zig-zags back to Henfield. Edge round the playing fields, then go right at the sports centre building. Continue through the children's play area and at the road cross left into Church Lane. Any path through the churchyard will take you to a terrace: the thatched **Cat House** is the last on the left. Keep ahead along Church Street and you will soon be back in the High Street.

POINTS OF INTEREST:
Mock Bridge – The Mock Bridge extension of the Adur Navigation was authorised in 1807. The wharf was constructed alongside the Henfield to Cowfold turnpike between the inn and bridge. The railway opened in 1861 and a year later the downstream Betley lock went 'out of repair'. The waterway was probably not re-opened. It is not known if barges were able to pass under the bridge to service the extinct Shermonbury flour mill, but an 1875 map shows a cut running north to Outlands Farm. This shows as a depression to the side of the modern road.
Cat House – The house is decorated below the eaves with a series of bird scarers depicting both a feline and feathered being. The story is that a wandering tom belonging to the Reverend Woodward made a meal of the owner's canary. A feud erupted between the two neighbours. Neither would back down so the house owner obtained effigies of Tom and Tweetie-Pie and arranged them so that they could be made to jangle as the vicar passed. The method of operation was by means of a stick emerging from a 'Zulu Hole'. This hole is still visible but its name is a mystery. In time the scarers were moved to their present positions.

The area around the Cat House is known as Pinchnose Green, the name no doubt deriving from the smells that were emitted from the tannery.

REFRESHMENTS:
The Bull, Mock Bridge.
There is a wide selection of inns in Henfield.

Walk 64   THE MARDEN CIRCUIT   8m (13km)

Maps: OS Sheets Landranger 197; Pathfinder 1286 and 1285.

A popular walk linking the four settlements. Plenty of ascents and descents, none too strenuous.

Start: At 808162, limited roadside parking in North Marden.

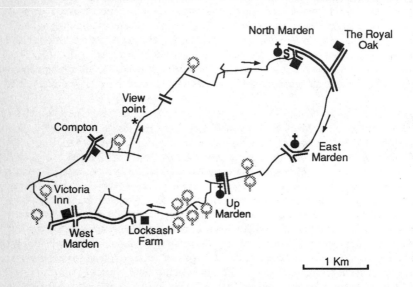

Walk to the main road (the B2141) and turn right along the wide grass verge. About 250 yards beyond the Hooksway turning, turn right through a gate on to a field path that crosses diagonally to a line of trees, then descends to **East Marden**. Just before the houses the line of the right of way is confused, so turn left on to a rough track to reach a road and go right to the village. At the thatched wellhouse turn into the North Marden road. Take the path opposite a white cottage, going through fields to a wooded hanger. Now go up a short, sharp climb to Up Marden. Turn left at the road, then right along a track towards the church. Detour left for the churchyard. Back on the track, cross a stile on the left, then go through a hedge and follow a wood edge towards an electricity pylon. Enter the wood and follow a well-defined track, ignoring the path on the left. In a newly planted area, on a downward slope, bear right on to an easily missed path – guidance has been chalked on a convenient tree. Climb to Locksash Farm and turn right there to walk down to West Marden and the Victoria Inn.

From the inn walk uphill between flint knapped walls and at a sharp bend turn right on a path that follows the fence of West Marden Hall. After some hillside walking beneath mature beech trees, cross a stile and walk up to a junction of paths. Go half-left across an open field, then through a penned scrubby area to reach Compton. In the village take the lane beside the Coach and Horses, passing the village school and then follow a bridleway into woodland. In 50 yards scramble right and up to exit the trees. Go left at the next crossing to traverse Telegraph Hill. Half-left from here **Uppark House** graces the skyline. Now descend to cross a road beside Bevis's Thumb, a Neolithic long barrow 150 feet in length. Climb gradually and take a path to the right, going alongside a wood edge. Zig-zag over two stiles and climb to a grassy gallop with the squashed hump of Apple Down prominent to the right. Turn left for 200 yards then cross a field to the corner of woodland. Go over a stile and descend through and beside a belt of trees to the valley bottom. Follow the path left for one final climb back to North Marden.

POINTS OF INTEREST:

East Marden – The Mardens, meaning hill boundaries, are four settlements isolated among the western Downs. Two, Up and North Marden can be considered as being two of Sussex's lost villages, now consisting of only the church and an adjoining farm. Changed medieval farming practices, possibly due to the Black Death, took a toll of their populations. Both of the small candlelit churches are worth a visit. St Michael's (13th-century) at Up Marden was probably a resting place on the pilgrim route from Winchester to Chichester. The largest of the four villages, West Marden, is the only one without a religious building, but it does have an inn.

Uppark House – The house was built in 1690 and was for decades the residence of the Featherstonehaugh family. Now in the care of the National Trust its interior was largely destroyed by fire in 1989. Luckily its art treasures were saved and a programme of restoration has been completed. Regrettably there is no right of way through its parkland.

REFRESHMENTS:
The Victoria Inn, West Marden.
The Royal Oak, Hooksway.

Maps: OS Sheets Landranger 197; Pathfinder 1305.
A level walk among the agricultural lands behind Bognor.
Start: At 938023, in the 'old road' 150 yards south of the Robin
Hood Inn, Shripney.

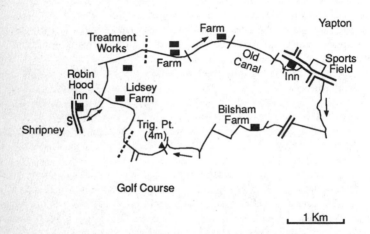

Cross the road, with care, and take a path opposite 'Peacehaven' into fields. Go around
glasshouses to a farm drive. Cross left on to a path to the entrance of the Southern
Water treatment works. Turn right on a track between fences. There is little evidence
here of the old **canal**, but once over the railway the earthworks are evident. Keep to
the top of the embankment because the canal bed has been transformed into a long
slurry pond. Beyond Church Farm the canal is well preserved. Where the earthworks
disappear, go over a crossing track to reach the edge of **Yapton**. Descend steps and
walk along the front of houses before entering a twitten. Emerge close to the main
road. (Turn left here for the **inn**.) Turn right and walk past the sports field. Turn right
again beside Maple Cottage and follow the power lines as they pass behind allotments.
Veer across a field to circle a clump of rubbish and join a wide track to a road. Turn

left for 100 yards, then cross and turn right on to a path by an overgrown hedge. The path scrambles into a deep ditch, then turns left along field edges before almost losing itself in an area dedicated to the cultivation of nettles, docks and thistles.

Thrash through, then turn right along a drive and after passing the farm cross open fields beside rifes (drainage ditches). Go left to reach an obvious footbridge and at the next junction turn right to reach a trig. pillar shaded by a solitary bush. Follow the path across the field to yet another rife and follow this around to a footbridge and the entry to a golf course. Slant over one fairway, and beyond the exit bridge bear right, across or round, a field to reach a planked bridge. Head for the white railway stile, cross the track and bear half-right to a gap in the hedge. Now trespass along the field edge to a signpost or struggle through a very overgrown right of way. Continue along a rutted track which follows the railway then bears left to Lidsey Farm. Continue to the nursery to join the outward route and reverse that back to the start.

POINTS OF INTEREST:

Canal – The Portsmouth and Arundel Canal was constructed as a barge canal from a junction with the Chichester Canal at Hunston to Ford on the River Arun. Opened in 1823 it was just 9 miles long and required only two locks. It was never a success, through traffic ceasing in 1840. The last commercial cargo was carried seven years later. Final closure was in 1856.

Yapton – Amongst old Sussex families the departure from a room without closing the door would earn the retort 'Were you born in Yapton?' Just inland from the coast the village was a centre of smuggling activities. The rear doors of the cottages involved were always left unlatched so that on the arrival of any excise men escape would be easy and undetected.

Inn – The name Shoulder of Mutton and Cucumber refers to an old Sussex dish of roast mutton with cucumber sauce. Part of this 200 year old hostelry was once used as the village mortuary, and in 1897 it received another claim to fame with the last recorded custom of wife selling. A local thatcher sold his spouse to a rat catcher who was lodging at the pub. The price was 7 shillings and 6 pence (37.5p) and a quart of ale!

REFRESHMENTS:
The Shoulder of Mutton and Cucumber, Yapton.

Walk 66   **PARHAM PARK**   8m (13km)

Maps: OS Sheets Landranger 197; Pathfinder 1287.

A walk across the wetlands to a deer park.

Start: At 053186, Lower Street car park, Pulborough.

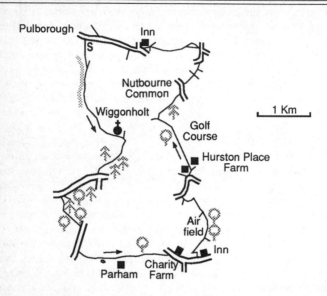

A lane to the right of the car park leads down to the water meadows: go ahead to the raised river bank and turn downstream. Cross a sluice and break away from the river to a stile beside a gate. Go over into an RSPB Reserve: the permitted paths are clearly marked, but the footpath crosses fields to join a track up to **Wiggonholt**. From the church, turn right towards the black building which houses the Reserve visitor centre. Cross the car park and follow a track through woodland to a road. Go right for $^1/_2$ mile. Two bridleways leave within 50 yards: take the second, which passes cottages to reach trees and a road. The lodges of **Parham Park** are just visible to the right. Enter the park through the white gates and follow the drive past the fish pond. Continue across grass to rejoin the drive before it leaves the park through two sets of gates. Opposite is **Charity Farm**, and the Crown Inn is straight ahead.

After visiting the inn return beside the front doors of Dukes Row and turn right into a caravan site. The exit is at the far end, beside the garages: cross a stream and turn left to continue among trees. Go around the airfield of the Southdown Gliding Club before bending to a tree-lined lane. Go right to Hurston Place Farm, turning left there to pass between the modern house and the outbuildings. Follow a track past the golf clubhouse, gaining a tarmac surface en route. At a bend, cross the fairways to reach a lone silver birch continuing to the end of a stand of Scots pine. Go down to a couple of footbridges and follow the stream to a road. Turn left and opposite a white cottage go right, up into the trees on Nutbourne Common. Cross a drive into a twitten, then maintain direction along a drive to reach a road. Turn right to a T-junction and there go left into a field which is usually partitioned by single wire electric fences. Walk towards the direction sign via the sturdier fence posts: the wires are broken beside many of these. There turn half-left to a stile and cross a garden to leave the property on the outside of the brick wall. Follow a track and unmade road to a lane that slopes left to join the main road beside the White Horse. Turn right, with care, along this busy road for 800 yards – luckily there is a wide footway which keeps you away from the traffic – to return to the start.

POINTS OF INTEREST:

Wiggonholt – The tiny church was originally built for the shepherds stationed on the water meadows, serving both as a shelter and place of worship. A sundial was built into the church wall, etched into a block on the south-west corner of the building just below head height. Curiously the church has no patron saint.

Parham Park – The manor of Parham was included in Domesday as the only manor in Sussex held by the Abbot of Westminster. The deer park supplied venison to London until the Dissolution in 1539. Queen Elizabeth I rested at the house en route to her stay at Cowdray. The present Elizabethan house was built in 1577 and restored in the early years of this century. Regrettably there is only one right of way through the park, but the house and gardens are open to the public (for a fee) each summer.

Charity Farm – This is still known to some old Storrington residents as Bread Farm. The name relates to two charities of 1779 and 1802 which supplied bread to poor families, who for various reasons were ineligible for parish relief. Land from the farm was given to provide the funds for the bread.

REFRESHMENTS:

The Crown Inn, Cootham.

There are numerous possibilities in Pulborough.

Maps: OS Sheets Landranger 198; Pathfinder 1306.

A walk through wild downland to visit an ancient hill fort.

Start: At 162080, a roadside parking area.

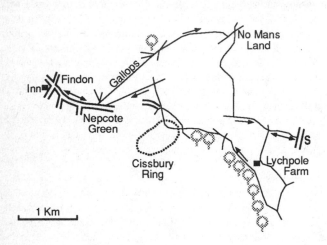

Enter the road used as a public path (RUPP) that extends westward from the car park and turn left at the first crossing path to pass between the attractive flint house and barns of Lychpole Farm. Continue on the concrete track and turn right at the end of the large storage sheds. Do not climb the hill: instead, make a second right turn to follow the base of the hill for nearly a mile. At first there is a choice of paths, low down beside a line of elder bushes, or a high track with a more open aspect. Both join beside the first fence. The trees on the left encroach and retreat, always keeping to the steeper slope, while to the right the open downland fields roll up to the northern crest. Ignore the first uphill path on offer, but in a few yards, beside a National Trust sign, turn up into the scrub. Entry to the **hill fort** is through a gate at the next path junction. At this point the Worthing conurbation spreads out before you to the south. Explore at will, but return to the trig. point. Now drop down off the summit towards the northwest (go left of a seat and solitary tree) where a stepped path leads down to a parking area and an information board.

Go ahead on a flint track, then turn left, the path soon slopes down to Findon village. The imposing cream faced building sitting above the racing stables is the Convent of our Lady of Sion – an unusual facade for a religious building. On reaching the road, go right – for those who do not wish to visit the fleshpots of Findon there are seats around the **green** where you can enjoy your snack. The thirsty ones must continue down Nepcot Lane for a further 600 yards to reach the village centre. Return to the green and cross left to a path junction. Climb the gate (it is usually chained) and continue up the centre of the field. Cross training gallops to enter a short fenced path. Go through a gate and bear half-right to a signpost prominent on the skyline. Recross the gallops to a meeting of tracks beside a clump of bushes. Now go ahead on a lonely track through wild downland, finally dropping to a tiny puddle in an area known as No Mans Land, one of several such names in this section of the downs. Turn right to wind along the valley bottom. At a crossing path go left back to the start, the last few yards retracing the outward route.

POINTS OF INTEREST:

Hill fort – Cissbury Ring is an Iron Age hill top fort second only in size to Maiden Castle in Dorset. Earlier Neolithic visitors left their mark with over 150 pock-like depressions indicating the central shaft of galleried flint mines. The Romans re-occupied the site towards the end of their occupation of Britain, probably as a defence station against marauding Saxon raiders. Years later it also featured in the county's defence, this time as a beacon site for the Spanish Armada.

Green – The annual September sheep fair held on Nepcote Green dates back to the 13th century. Traditionally it was held on the 14th day of the month, but this has now been changed to the second Saturday. Besides being a commercial event, when many thousand sheep changed hands, it was also a social occasion for the smock-coated downsmen who had delivered their charges from many remote farms. No doubt many pints were sunk in the local hostelries. The coming of the railway to Steyning brought increased business. Flocks from all over southern England could now reach Findon via this new railhead and downland tracks. Today multi-decked transporters disgorge straight into the pens.

REFRESHMENTS:
The Gun Inn, Findon.

Walk 68   FRESHFIELD   8m (13km)

Maps: OS Sheets Landranger 198; Pathfinder 1268.

An easy walk to a bargeman's rest.

Start: At 349258, the wilderness car park, Lindfield.

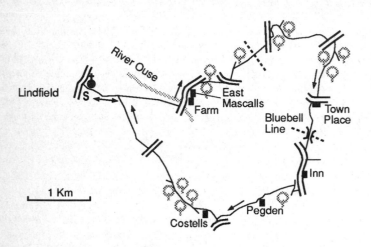

Make your way through the pedestrian exit towards the church, turn right into the close then go over a stile into a twitten which soon converts to a fenced path. Beside the buildings, keep ahead towards the golf course, you are safe from wayward balls for you follow the river bank, to the right, to Mascalls Bridge. Turn left along the road, passing the **farm**, and just beyond the golf club entrance, go right through a copse. In the field beyond, first follow the fence, then ease away, clipping a small stone shed before bisecting two barns and joining a road. Walk straight ahead, then, beside the cottages, go left on a farm track. Fork right into a field, cross the footbridge and enter a band of trees pungent with the smell of wild garlic. Cross the Bluebell Line (see Note to Walk 62) and veer half-right through a series of paddocks to a lane. Turn left, then go right into the adjoining field. Walk parallel to the road, then turning right behind a pair of completely demolished cottages and into woodland. Dip to a bridge, then climb through a wood. After crossing a field, follow the edge of a shrubbery to a lane.

The next path is visible to the left. At the first bend break right and slowly descend through trees and fields to a road at Town Place. Go right for a few yards then left on a path that keeps to the garden hedge before crossing to a derelict bridge. As you re-cross the railway a white building shows ahead: aim for it, it will take you to the **Sloop Inn**. From the inn, go uphill and turn right through a gap towards a wood. Double back right, then, at a path junction, go left along paddock rails. Walk through a bluebell wood to a stile. Pass below Pegden, follow the drive and return to fields just beyond Nash House. Follow an access drive to a road, but turn back on another metalled way into Costells. Bear right along a short avenue of trees and right again in the wood. Now follow the power lines down to a wet area and fork right there to leave the trees. Cross in front of Keepers Cottage and a series of 'squeezers' takes you to the drive for Walstead Forge. The path finds its way round the buildings, and crosses a stream before joining a concrete farm road. In the dip, on the left, is a clump of red dogwood – a brilliant colour before the leaves appear. Rejoin the outward route and turn left for a 10 minutes reverse of the outward route back to **Lindfield** and the start.

POINTS OF INTEREST:

Farm – East Mascalls house is early 16th century, but was much enlarged in 1896. The decoratively arranged panel struts around the front porch are, for Sussex, an uncommon form of embellishment.

Sloop Inn – The inn has been converted from two bargeman's cottages which stood on a canalised section of the Ouse Navigation and served the waterway for 70 years after the opening in 1799. A few steps to the north, upstream of the road bridge is the chamber of Freshfield Lock. Prior to the Second World War a humped backed bridge carried the road over the canal, as the traffic increased this obstacle had to go.

Lindfield – Two of the village's many interesting buildings stand adjacent to the north side of the church. Old Place contains a small Manor house, said to have once been a country cottage belonging to Queen Elizabeth I. All is not genuine, however, as much was added in Victorian times. Next door is another reputedly historic house, this one claiming to have originally been a hunting lodge of Henry VIII.

REFRESHMENTS:

The Sloop Inn, Freshfield.
There are numerous possibilities in Lindfield.

Walk 69   SOUTHWICK HILL   8m (13km)

Maps: OS Sheets Landranger 198; Pathfinder 1288 and 1307.

An initial climb, then an easy walk on wide tracks.

Start: At 232114, a small parking area to the side of the 'Springs' buildings.

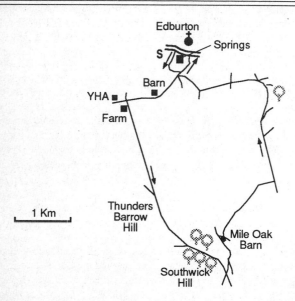

From the car park climb a ladder and steps to enter the National Trust area known as the Fulking Escarpment. This is the only steep climb of the walk. At the path junction, turn right, then go through a gate to join the South Downs Way (SDW). Follow the Way, a wide flint track, past a barn and a set of radio masts, then, beside a cluster of houses, go left to a farm. Walk past the farm and greyhound paddocks, continuing through superb country, populated with skylarks in spring and summer, and offering fine views..

Enjoy the views as you descend pleasantly. After passing an enclosure and a departing path, the track appears less used: rise slightly over Thundersbarrow Hill, on which are the still visible remnants of ancient earthworks. Resume the descent to reach Southwick Hill, another National Trust enclosure. Go through bushes and on returning into the open, go left through a gate. At a crossing path, double back left, following the Sussex Border Path (SBP) signs to Mile Oak Barn, passing above the mouth of the **A27 tunnel**, then negotiating a less than salubrious field corner.

Turn right at the barn, and after 50 yards follow the SBP (East Sussex version) left along a track that climbs steadily. Go left at a junction for a long straight walk to a crest. Once through the gate, on Fulking Down, head for the left-hand edge of a clump of thorn. Just prior to the trees, go left to rejoin the SDW beside a Bronze Age barrow. The penned area on the left was the site of the Fulking Isolation Hospital. Various paths now lead off to the right: ignore these, keeping beside a fence to follow the Way back to **Edburton Hill**.

Turn right through a familiar gate, but instead of reversing the outward route, remain on the bridleway as it winds off the hill. At the bottom, back-track for a short distance then turn to the road. Cross to reach a path above the tarmac which leads to the church entrance. It is now just a few yards along the narrow lane back to the '**Springs**'.

POINTS OF INTEREST:

A27 tunnel – The tunnel taking the western section of the Brighton bypass, the A27, under Southwick Hill was a victory for the conservationists. The original plan was for the usual cut and slash through the Downs. The hill, a large portion of which is owned by the National Trust, is regarded by the coastal communities as their 'bit of space'. They and the countryside agencies combined to present a formidable argument at the extended enquiry and, for once, the success was theirs.

'**Springs**' – A Sussex backwater is not the place where you expect to find the largest family-owned smokery in southern England. Springs Smoked Salmon was founded in 1964 in some redundant farm buildings. The owner learnt his trade from a Norfolk relative, and the intricacies of the process remain a well kept secret. If the shop is open, why not treat yourself and see if your palette can identify the smoking ingredient.

Edburton Hill – Edburton is Eadburge's farmstead, Eadburge being the granddaughter of King Alfred the Great who founded the settlement in the 10th century. The original church was built around 960AD, the present building – which is believed to have used some of the earlier materials – about two centuries later. The church houses a lead font, one of only three in existence in Sussex. The font has had an eventful life: during the Civil War it was despoiled by Cromwell's soldiers who used it as a horse trough.

REFRESHMENTS:
The Shepherd and Dog, Fulking, about 1 mile to the east of 'Springs'.

Walk 70   **GRAFFHAM**   8m (13km)

Maps: OS Sheets Landranger 197; Pathfinder 1286.
Horses and Heathland says it all.
Start: At 949187, the National Trust car park, Lavington
Common.

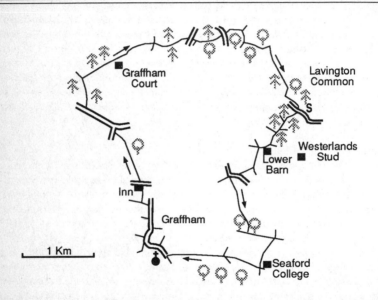

Cross the road, go over the stile beside the wooden gate and enter a plantation of
conifers. Keep ahead to a pair of cottages, where a track leads left to **Westerlands Stud**,
the roof of which is just visible. Go through the Lower Barn complex and curve round
beside a practice polo-ground. Turn right, beside a modern house, into a hazel wood
and right again when a lane is reached. Walk to a sharp bend and go left over a stile.
The footpath crosses a drive and remains between fences before veering half-left over
two sets of planks into a wood. Turn left on the next strip of metalling, then follow a
road used as a public path (RUPP) to the buildings of Seaford College. At the cross
path, turn right for an easy under-down stroll to estate gates at the end of the straggling
village of **Graffham**. Go right, passing the **church** and noting Stowberry Cottage with

134

its semi-detached chimney. Turn into the field opposite Guillards Cottages then go right through scrub to the White Horse Inn.

A path leaves from the front of the inn: follow signs through fields and a copse, heading generally north-west. On reaching a lane, step right to a T-junction and bear left there. About 80 yards beyond Topleigh Cottage, go right into a wood of rhododendron and larch. The next path, still in the trees, departs right: it widens and deteriorates as it runs behind Graffham Court. Follow an inter-field fence to a crossing gate, go through and turn half-right to the corner of pines. Go left, away from the main track, and after battling past a large clump of bamboo cross into another section of wooded heathland. Keep ahead, ignoring all side paths, signed or not to reach a lane. Go over to an unmade farm drive. Before the buildings, go right, back into the trees. Take the left fork, a semi-surfaced track, which after an open section is downgraded to that of a woodland horse path. Cross a drive into the National Trust area and at the first opportunity follow the horseshoe waymark right. Finally, swing parallel to the road to reach the rear of the car park.

POINTS OF INTEREST:

Westerlands Stud – The area of the walk has a long association with horses, stud farms and the racing industry. One recent character was Florence Nagle, of Westerlands Stud, who for years battled with the authorities for the recognition of women trainers. Whilst waging this fight, and in order to circumnavigate the ban, all of her horses were entered under the name of her head lad.

Graffham – The village has a resident ghost, a young lady standing by a well. She is the wife of a young, early Georgian squire, Gorton Orme. He dallied with a local beauty and subsequently starved his spouse to death. Locals believed that the emaciated body was dumped down a well but the squire produced a coffin which was buried in the family vault. In 1840 during alterations the coffin was revealed. The rector surprised by the weight ordered it to be opened. It contained stones not bones.

Church – St Giles' church is an attractive flint-knapped building. Its early Norman font is one of six imported in to Sussex as a 'job-lot' by William I. Another ancient feature is the 13th-century vestry door. Many books on Sussex make great play of open lock on the inner side, but in fact little of the original now remains. The 'King and Bishop' key which operated the lock was stolen from the church several years ago. A replica of the key resides in the Victoria and Albert Museum.

REFRESHMENTS:
The White Horse Inn, Graffham.

Maps: OS Sheets Landranger 187; Pathfinder 1246.
A walk brushing against the Roman road of Stane Street.
Start: At 117316, the lane beside Slinfold Church.

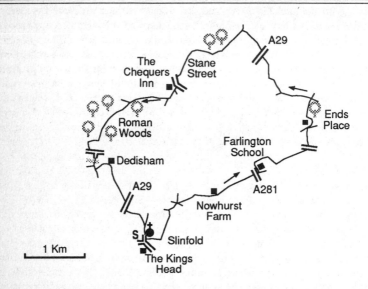

Enter the churchyard by the Horsham-tiled lychgate, cross the front of the church and continue through an extension to reach a path across fields. Turn left by the farm buildings on to a track which rises, then falls to a river. Cross a bridge and turn right for Nowhurst Farm. There are several paths here, but follow the drive (a bridleway) to reach a road (the A281) almost opposite Farlington School. Cross, with care, and take the bridleway which skirts the school, passing a pond and continuing along an enclosed track and woodland path to Strood Lane. Beside South Lodge, opposite, another bridleway eases down to the ornate, mock Georgian apology that is Ends Place. Ignore the footpath on the right, following the bridleway as it rounds an ornamental pond. On entering woodland, take the higher and drier path through the trees. At the first crossing path turn left, and in the third field cross diagonally half-right to a copse and the paddocks of Westbrook Lea. Follow the signs and stiles to a driveway, then go past Westbrook Hall and cross a Bailey Bridge to reach the A29. Turn right, with care, for 170 yards then go left along the drive of Charmons Farm.

Where the drive diverges, take the left-hand farm track, turning left at the buildings into a large open field. Follow the hedge on the right and where it ends, bear half-right into woodland. On emerging from the wood turn right. The trees in front cover the route of the Roman road, but on reaching Stane Street we hear no sound of the legion's tramping feet, only the noise from aircraft using Gatwick's Runway 28. Continue to a road and turn left for **the Chequers Inn**. From the inn walk south along the lane turning right along the side of the timber-framed Burnt House on to a horse-indented bridleway. In a little under $^1/_2$ mile turn left on to a footpath which slips down through Roman Woods to meet a wide track. Turn left and go down past Furnace Farm to reach a road. The way to **Dedisham** can now be seen 80 yards to the left. Next, cross the River Arun and from the farm buildings follow the drive past a house and school to reach Stane Street again. The road is now followed by the A29 Bognor road. Unfortunately Dedisham House hides behind high hedges, but in the field opposite, the earthworks of a filled-in pond can be readily traced. Cross the A29 with great care and go right to reach a path, on the left, which leads across fields towards white cottages. On reaching these, turn right up the lane back to the church.

POINTS OF INTEREST:

The Chequers Inn – Although sporting a game-board inn sign, the inn is more likely named after the 'chequer' or wild service tree, the tree being the sign of an inn during Roman times. Rowhook where the inn is situated is on the junction of two Roman roads. Stane Street (Chichester to London) is definable for much of its length, long stretches of it having been usurped by the modern A29. The un-named branch road from here to Farmley Heath near Wonersh has disappeared without a trace – barely a hedgerow exists along its line.

Dedisham – This is an ancient moated agricultural settlement, once a self-sufficient community adjacent to Stane Street, the Roman posting house at Alfoldene, and the River Arun. The original house was granted a licence to castellate in 1271 but was sacked by Cromwell's men in 1643. The house on the site today is probably a wing of a 16th-century house.

REFRESHMENTS:
The Kings Head, Slinfold.
The Chequers Inn, Rowhook.

Walk 72   A FOOT INTO HAMPSHIRE   8½m (13½km)

Maps; OS Sheets Landranger 197; Pathfinder 1285.

An easy downland walk in country more akin to its western neighbour.

Start: At 773136, the lay-by at the cross-roads on the edge of West Marden village.

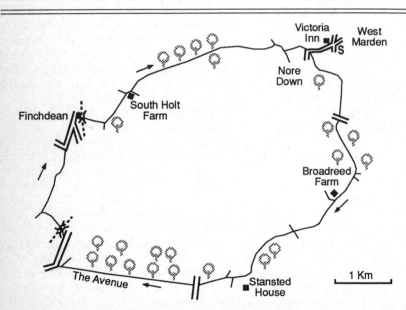

Walk uphill past the Victoria Inn and turn left on to the lower of the two footpaths beside Noredown House. This path plays with the edge of a beechwood before crossing a lane on to a bridleway above **Big Busto House**. Climb steadily and leave the wood beside a pair of flint faced cottages. Continue ahead on a stony track that becomes a metalled drive at Broadreed Farm. Visible among the farm buildings is an old granary set on saddlestones. Follow a driveway for over a mile, passing **Stansted House**, to meet a road at a pillared gate house. Cross on to **The Avenue** and enjoy this peaceful perambulation on smooth short grass to its end. Now go down through trees, pass a forest information board and get your passport ready, for at the road a Hampshire signpost confirms that you have crossed the county border.

138

Turn right along the road. A double signpost opposite gnome-infested No. 73 indicates a path, to the left, which crosses the railway. At the next set of buildings a new waymark appears, the deer's head emblem of the Staunton Way. Turn right on to an ancient open field track (Wellsworth Lane) that bears no resemblance to its name. Idsworth 'new' house is prominent to the left. At the road go downhill to reach the George Inn at Finchdean. A footpath beside the inn goes under the railway and rises back into Sussex. Continue along the field edge to meet a drive closing from the right. Turn left for South Holt Farm. The right of way goes between the farmhouse and outbuildings – a stone mounting block sits on the grass verge by the farm. Ignore side paths and walk towards the corner of a wood, firstly along a flint track, then along a headland path. Cross right on to a path which undulates along the edge of woods before striking into the trees on a wider track. Now go through fields to reach an abandoned farm. Turn right on to a bridleway, then go left at the next junction to drop down into West Marden.

POINTS OF INTEREST:

Big Busto House – This curious name derives from a Roman farmstead and burial ground discovered in the area. A preliminary dig unearthed the buildings of Busto Mephar whilst further excavations revealed the skeleton of a child buried within the confines, it being common Roman practice for the body of a child to be buried beneath the floor of its home to avoid disturbance by wild animals.

Stanstead House – The house is relatively modern, but is the third house on the site having been built in the early years of this century after the previous one was largely destroyed by fire in 1900. Remains of the fire-razed ruin were used in the building of the chapel to the south-west of the present house. Defoe, during a visit to Stansted in 1724, enthused that from the dining room window he was not only able to see the magnificent avenue of beeches but also Portsmouth, Spithead and the Isle of Wight.

The Avenue – This is a wide grassy ride flanked by beech trees, stretching from Stansted House almost to Rowlands Castle. The trees were originally laid out early in the 18th century, but replanted in 1820. Now sadly past their prime they have succumbed to disease and the 1987 storm, but the ride is still a firm favourite with locals.

REFRESHMENTS:

The Victoria Inn, West Marden.
The George Inn, Finchdean.

Walk 73   **BOXGROVE AND HALNAKER**   8¹/₂m (13¹/₂km)
Maps: OS Sheets Landranger 197; Pathfinder 1286 and 1305.
An ancient 12th-century priory and a Roman road.
Start: At 939107, the car park at Eartham Woods.

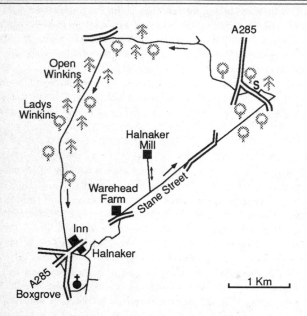

From the car park, turn right along the road for 200 yards, then go left on a chalky
track to the A285. Cross, with care, and, just before a farm, turn right across a field to
a stile. Go over and bear half-left to the end of a hedgerow. Halnaker Mill stands on a
knoll away to the left. Walk beside trees and scrub to a path through woods, continuing
to a clearing beside a road. Turn back left along a flint track and, beside a gate, go
right, back into the trees. This long straight track through the woodland has unusual
names, Open and Ladys Winkins, and is usually muddy on its lower section. Ignore
any side tracks to emerge into a meadow beside a flint wall. Follow the wall past a
farm and houses to the road junction at Halnaker. Turn right away from the houses to
reach a field path, on the left, which aims for Boxgrove Priory to reach the A285
which follows Roman Stane Street. Cross, and walk to another road. Turn right, and

140

in the village centre, opposite a telephone box, go left along Church Lane to the **church** and ruined **priory**.

Take the footpath beside the church, going half-left across the first field, then turning north along an avenue of young trees. Turn left, then right on a path beside garden boundaries. Another tree lined path now leads to a drive: side step right to a stile beside a gate and continue to reach the A285 at Warehead Farm. Cross and follow Stane Street (the modern road leaves it for a time here) which, beyond the buildings, appears as a sunken track. Where this track ends, climb up Halnaker Hill on a dead end footpath to the **mill**. The all round view justifies the extra effort involved. Return to Stane Street where you may encounter a little difficulty in following the Roman line as the next section receives little use. However, once over a metal ladder stile things improve. Beside a parking area, rejoin the road and follow it, with care, up a rise. The second footpath on the left, at a bend in the road, proclaims 'Stane Street' on its direction post. Follow it, passing further haphazard signposts. The path soon re-enters the trees and weaves from side to side on the raised track. Cross a road into Forestry Commission woodland and immediately opposite a National Trust information plaque turn left twice to regain the car park.

POINTS OF INTEREST:

Church – The first recorded date of cricket in Sussex was at Boxgrove in 1622, the churchyard apparently being used as a practice pitch. A grave in the south-east corner of the churchyard is of Pilot Officer W (Billy) Fiske. Born in Chicago he died after a German raid on Tangmere airfield, and is honoured as the first United States citizen to be killed on active service in World War II.

Boxgrove Priory – The Priory was built in the 12th century as a Benedictine house under the French abbey of Lessoy. The Der La Warr chantry was built as a fine memorial chapel to a local who died in 1526.

Halnaker Mill – This is the oldest tower mill in Sussex, at 420 feet high. It was the feudal mill of the Goodwood Estates, and with its unhindered position collected wind from all quarters and was worked hard. The earliest recorded mill on the site is in 1540, though the present one was probably built around 1750. Its outer fabric was restored in 1934 but the inside remains a void. Due to its prominent position it makes a useful landmark for coastal shipping.

REFRESHMENTS:

The Angelsey Arms, Halnaker.

Walk 74   WEPHAM DOWN   8½m (13½km)

Maps: OS Sheets Landranger 197; Pathfinder 1287 and 1306.
An open downland walk with wide open views.
Start: At 071125, Parham Post, reached by a single track road
from the B2139.

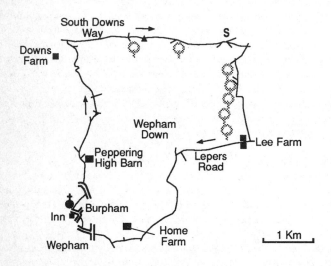

Turn left along the South Downs Way and at the next junction (before the top of the rise), go right to a scrubby hedge. Pass through this hedge to cross to the end of a long plantation of trees. Walk down the left-hand side of the trees: a signpost points the right of way as it veers away left, but the used route is to follow the track as it breaks left, then turns right down to Lee Farm. Turn right between the farm buildings and follow the **Pest Track** as it eases up to Wepham Down. Where the track turns right, break left beside the training gallop into the valley bottom. This is pleasant grassland walking at first, then a typical rutted way develops. At the top of a slight incline, cross the gallops (two stiles) and climb to join the concrete access road from Home Farm. Continue on this drive down into Wepham. At the road turn right for a few yards, then go left at a junction, walking down through a mixture of buildings. At the bottom of the slope go up the bank to reach a stile and field path to Burpham. On this path the local council have found a use for their redundant kerb stones! Rejoin the road, going left for the village centre and the George and Dragon Inn.

Enter the churchyard and turn right beside the wall, then follow the field edge to a road. Here go left, uphill, then right to Peppering High Barn. The path skirts the buildings and continues as a bridleway, climbing gently towards a triangular group of trees. Fork right, then turn left through the clump and out into open fields. Cross a road used as a public path (RUPP) and drop steeply to the floor of a coombe. The climb out is equally sharp, and as this northern face is used as an overwintering pasture for cattle the going is not good. Follow the track as it continues above Downs Farm to join the South Downs Way at another messy cattle stance. The last 2 miles of the walk are along the Way. Climb to the top of Amberley Mount: from the ridge the views are an ample reward for the effort expended. From this height the drainage system of the Wild Brooks (see Note to Walk 50) becomes apparent, and there is a birds eye view of Parham House and Park. Go over **Rackham Hill**, through Springhead Clump and back to the start.

POINTS OF INTEREST:

Pest Track – The Pest Track, or Leper's Road, runs westwards from Lee Farm, before falling down Perry Hill to Burpham. In medieval times there was a leper settlement near the present farm site. The residents, being barred from local churches, were forced to worship across the river at a long lost chapel at Offham. The track was their route to worship, but it is unclear how they crossed the river, the Arun then being wider and stronger than today.

Rackham Hill – Rackham Banks, on the hill, is an, as yet, unexplained series of earthworks. Most certainly connected to early habitation, the hill was sporadically occupied until the 1930s when a family of flint pickers finally left their dwellings for a more amenable climate. It is believed that these huts were in the trees to the south of the walk. Nothing remains as during World War II they were used for target practice and completely destroyed.

REFRESHMENTS:
The George and Dragon Inn, Burpham.

Walk 75   WANDER TO WASHINGTON $8^1/_2$m ($13^1/_2$km)

Maps: OS Sheets Landranger 198; Pathfinder 1287.
An underdown walk to a popular inn.
Start: At 179112, Fletcher's Croft car park, Steyning.

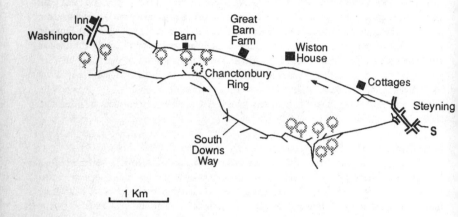

Go to the right of the Steyning Centre, taking School Lane to Church Street. The old buildings of the grammar school are on the left. Turn right into the High Street shopping area and, beyond the Star, on a sharp bend, cross to Mouse Lane. This narrow road collects the water flowing from the Downs, so after a period of heavy rain you are going against the tide. Go past cottages and over a rise, then break left through a hedge on to a field path that joins a track skirting the grounds of **Wiston House**. Continue through the aptly named Great Barn Farm, keeping to the right of Malt House and nudging into a wood. Pass a lonely barn and climb a few feet before falling back to a junction of paths. Cross a field (heading roughly north-west) and bear half-left along the south side of a hedge. At the end of the farm, turn right on a path to the Frankland Arms. Note the privy, still resident in the garden of the house on the left.

Now walk towards the Downs. The third path on the left (opposite Stocks Mead) climbs through trees to the South Downs Way. Turn left, but 100 yards beyond the gas reducing station leave the way through a gate on the left. Climb out of the disused pit and follow old fence posts across the open downland, with superb views over the Weald to the North Downs and back into Hampshire. Pass a dew pond to rejoin the main track as it goes round **Chanctonbury Ring**. To the east of the ring the view extends to East Sussex: the white chimney is the last survivor of Shoreham Power Station. Go over the first crossing track, collect a bridleway coming in from the right, and turn left at the next junction. Go along the top of the scarp, ignoring the first downhill path but moving off the field edge into the trees. Turn left on the next path offered to begin a long descent to Steyning. At a fork, keep right on the footpath. Join a track beside the allotments and on reaching a road keep to the right of the factory. Go around to a row of flint cottages, where an opening opposite No. 37 leads back to the High Street. It is now just a short step back to the start.

POINTS OF INTEREST:
Wiston House – Now a conference centre, this Elizabethan manor was built in 1576 by Sir Thomas Shirley. His two sons Anthony and Robert were politely known as 'adventurers'. As local iron masters they traded in the illegal export of arms without licence. Canons reached Persia, where Robert, who had married a local lady, was adviser to the Shah. Brother Anthony was one claimant to the authorship of Shakespeare's plays!

Chanctonbury Ring – The 'ring' truly refers to the Neolithic earthworks, although the clump of trees is usually afforded the name. The pre-historic site, which also contains a Romano-Celtic temple within its ring, was probably connected with the fort at Cissbury, just to the south. The trees were planted by a young Charles Goring of Wiston House in 1760. It is said he daily carried water up ensuring their successful establishment on the chalk. He survived into his eighties so was able to enjoy their increasing prominence on the landscape. The site was storm devastated and there has been much replanting, but the result will not be evident for many years.

REFRESHMENTS:
The Frankland Arms, Washington.
There are numerous possibilities in Steyning.

Walk 76   FINDON AND WASHINGTON $8\frac{1}{2}$m ($13\frac{1}{2}$km)

Maps: OS Sheets Landranger 198; Pathfinder 1306 and 1287.
A downland walk along both sides of the Washington Gap.
Start: At 122088, the centre of Findon village.

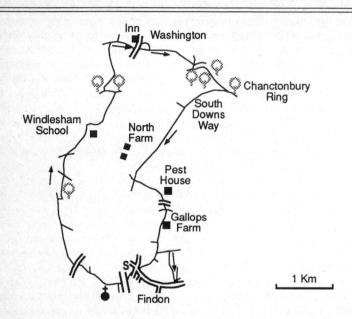

Walk past the Gun Inn and, beside **Findon** village hall, a path leads over a field to the A24. Cross, with care, into the drive of Findon Place. At the church go right through a kissing gate and along a path beside the edge of a wood. Go over two stiles to a road above the cricket field. Follow this road used as a public path (RUPP) rising, then falling to a cross track. Turn right for 60 yards, then go left along the edge of woodland. Follow a hedge, then, above Highden Barn, step right on to a track that falls to the Windlesham School complex. As you round on the driveway, on the left, among the rubbish, is an old hand-operated petrol pump. Opposite the sports field bear left up a track to reach a metalled section of the South Downs Way (SDW) above Washington Bostal. The old English word bostal, indicates a hill path, so go uphill. The surface ends at a gate: drop right into the trees on a steep path that is the alternate route for

146

the SDW. Leave the trees to join a wooden fence above the earthworks of the A24. The fence leads to a farm bridge. Cross, walk past Washington church and at the T-junction turn left for the Frankland Arms.

Ignore the path opposite the inn, returning along the road for 150 yards. Go left, cross a stream, pass a farm and then veer across a field to a junction of paths below the hill. Turn right for 80 yards then left into the trees. Now climb up, with stops to admire the view back over the Weald. You clear the trees beside Chanctonbury Ring: turn right along the SDW, but nip over to look at the dew pond. Now where the Way turns right, keep ahead. The overbridge below North Farm is a new piece of furniture for the Worthing road. Go left at the crossing track towards the farm in the valley bottom. Before the cottage (The Pest House) break up across a field to a gate. Cross the lane beyond and follow a track to Gallops Farm. As you walk down the drive you may see horses outlined on the skyline gallops. At the houses there is a choice: follow the road to the village or turn left, then right on to a bridleway that divides the stables from the gallops. At the green turn right to return to the start.

POINTS OF INTEREST:

Dew pond – The Chanctonbury dew pond is relatively recent, having been dug in 1870 and restored 100 years later by the Society of Sussex Downsmen. The ponds were constructed as oases where shepherds could water their sheep. A pit was dug six feet deep and lined with straw covered with wet clay. The straw provided insulation against the rising heat of the earth at night, thus keeping the surface of the pond cool, and causing the moisture in the air to condense into the water.

Findon – Although Findon has a long connection with sheep, it is really a community devoted to the horse. The village sign depicts a horse and jockey and in the small range of shops there are several with an equine slant. At one time there was enough trade in the area to support three village forges. The downland turf is well drained and provides what is almost an all-weather surface. The main stables, to the east of the village, were built in the mid-thirties and were once the home of the famous 'jump' trainer Ryan Price.

REFRESHMENTS:

The Gun Inn, Findon.
The Frankland Arms, Washington.
There are also possibilities in Findon.

Walk 77   ALBOURNE AND TWINEHAM   8½m (13½km)

Maps: OS Sheets Landranger 198; Pathfinder 1288.

An easy walk in the flatlands west of the Brighton road.

Start: At 264168, a lay-by near the school entrance at the north end of The Street, Albourne.

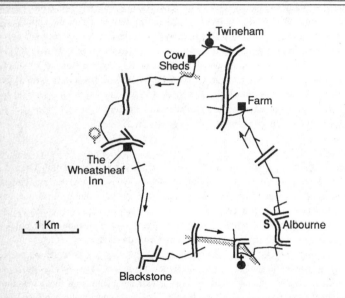

Walk back to join the B2116 by **Pound Cottage**. Cross right, and go between the barns to follow a track to a junction. Fork left on a wide grass path: there are now wide views to the north; Blackdown, above Haslemere, shows up half-left. Walk down to a road. Cross beside the battery farm complex and follow field edges northwards. Keep to the left of the cottages to join a semi-surfaced access drive. Circle a pond and continue to a road. Turn right. It is ³/₄ mile to the next turning, but traffic is light. At the cluster of houses that is **Twineham**, follow the sign, left, to the school and church.

Go past the church, then cross diagonally to large cow barns. Go ahead on a track through a graveyard of farm equipment before turning right along the riverbank. A few yards beyond a pylon, go left to a stile, cross and maintain direction beside hedgerows, joining a bridleway for the final stretch to a road. Turn left and at the farther end of the causewayed bridge follow the track to the right. Bear away from the stream and, where the track narrows, break left along field edges to reach a road. The Wheatsheaf Inn is to the left.

It may be difficult to leave this friendly inn: when you do, take the adjacent path and walk towards the Downs. At **Stockmans** in Blackstone, turn left along a road, and where it bends, go right, around the cottages, into fields. Bisect a pair of barns and go up to farm buildings. Go left along lane and take the second path on the right, beyond the phone box. Cross two footbridges and follow an overgrown ditch to a farm. Now follow the farm's access drive to a road.

Here you have a choice of routes: a damp walk leads off opposite the Old School, but for a drier walk go right to the church. Take the path beside the Lawsonnii hedge and continue to a footbridge. Cross and turn left on a bank, then break right below the houses. Go right on a crossing path and follow The Street back to the start. As you wander down this Albourne road ponder on the reasons for some of the house names.

POINTS OF INTEREST:

Pound Cottage – The animal pound attached to the cottage of the same name belonged to the Manor of Albourne, it was used in the 17th century as a restraining pen for wayward beasts. The owners were obliged to pay a fee for their release. An original idea of wheel clamping? The pound was restored in 1987.

Twineham – Twineham church is one of only two in West Sussex built from Tudor bricks. At first glance the walls seem too light to support the heavy roof constructed of Horsham slates. To the left of the churchyard gates is an area devoid of monuments, this being a Quaker burial plot. It was in service from 1694 until 1732 during which time 56 members of the Society were interred. A tablet refers to the purchase of the ground, but one story is that it was a gift from the vicar. His daughter had married a member of the following and he was concerned that on her death her body would have been buried in unconsecrated soil.

Stockmans – This ancient house at Blackstone was originally the village 'local', but smuggling brought in a greater income than the sale of alcohol. Some time in the 17th century the excise men finally caught up with the entrepreneurs. The licence was withdrawn, the inn closed and the house became a private residence.

REFRESHMENTS:
The Wheatsheaf Inn, Wheatsheaf Road, Woodmancote.

Walk 78   LECONFIELD LANDS   9m (14^1/$_2$km)
Maps: OS Sheets Landranger 197; Pathfinder 1266.
A walk through estate lands and adjacent farms and villages.
Start: At 966239, Petworth Park car park.

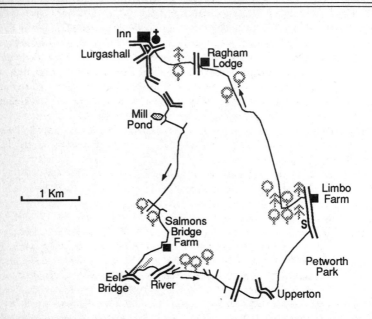

Return to the road and turn left for 500 yards. Opposite Limbo Farm re-enter the park through the white gate beside the lodge. Go right, as signed, along a long, wide ride and across the head of a large pond. Once over the first of many cattle grids, rise slightly towards a group of barns. The eastern flanks of Blackdown show prominently. At a fork, keep left towards the woods: in autumn this area is overpopulated with inexperienced pheasants – it is a very different story in the new year. Leave the estate by Ragham Lodge turning right for 80 yards on to a path through fields and a copse to arrive unexpectedly at Lurgashall, via the local football pitch. Within the village there is a picture postcard village green, encompassed by the **church**, inn and shop. Make your way to the signpost at the corner of the green and walk along the unmarked road beside Signpost Cottage. At a sharp bend hoist yourself into a field and on reaching tarmac turn right to Lurgashall Mill Pond. There is no mill building as this has been moved to The Weald Open Air Museum at Singleton.

Turn left beside the farm buildings, then cross a stile and continue rightwards. Temporarily join a track to pass another pond, then head towards power lines and woodland. Turn left outside the trees and follow a track, right, into a field where the path is rarely re-instated. Cross a pocket of the field to follow headlands to Salmons Bridge Farm. Go straight across the drive, then look for a stile half hidden in a dip. Follow the River Lod along the valley bottom as far as Eel Bridge and there cross the stream to bear left, uphill. At the top of the slope the path turns towards the hamlet of River. At a road, turn left and after 100 yards, go right up a stepped path which crosses a track and continues upwards on a hillside still littered with the remains of the 1987 storm. At a path junction below a house, turn right along the azalea-edged drive. Go over a cattle grid and up a grassy slope to follow a path that gives excellent views of the downland ridge from Beacon Hill to Chanctonbury. Turn left along a sunken track to enter Upperton (Upper Tillington), then go right, downhill. Just beyond a bend, drop left into a twitten where a door in a wall allows access into **Petworth Park**. From here the car park is away to the left, on a bearing of 30°.

POINTS OF INTEREST:

Church – Lurgashall church has an unusual 16th-century timber gallery built on to the southern wall. This was originally intended as a shelter where worshippers from outlying farms could, in inclement weather, between matins and evensong, eat their victuals in some semblance of comfort. Later it became the village school, then the vestry. The large stone in the porch was placed on top of newly occupied graves as a deterrent to body snatchers.

Petworth Park – This 738 acre deer park was designed by Capability Brown. He spent several years developing the area for which he received the sum of £5,600. The painter Turner was a regular visitor to the park and many of his paintings are now on display in the house. The sculpture at the edge of the upper lake was commissioned by the third Earl of Egremont as a monument to one of his favourite hounds which had drowned there.

REFRESHMENTS:
The Noahs Ark, Lurgashall.

Walk 79   SINGLETON   9m (14½km)

Maps: OS Sheets Landranger 197; Pathfinder 1286.
A downland walk recommended for autumn colour.
Start: At 875166, the car park at Cocking Hill.

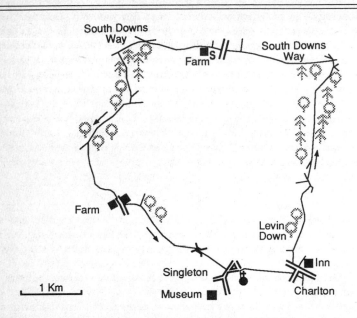

The car park is a chilly place especially if a northerly wind is blowing, so get your boots on and turn left along the South Downs Way. Beyond the farm this chalky track begins to climb Cocking Down. At the first crossing path turn left to reach the trees above Warren Bottom, then go left again into a coniferous wood. There are now many side paths but the right of way is adequately marked: if in doubt, keep ahead and continue to lose height. About 50 yards after a bridleway joins, cross a wide track and begin to descend more steeply. At the edge of the trees the long spur of Bow Hill looms ahead: turn left once again, down to an isolated house and walk up to a farm and road end.

Take the path beside the cottages and go over a stile opposite a decrepit hut. Beyond the reservoir there are views through the trees to West Dean House and down the Lavant valley. Next, as you drop down towards **Singleton**, the widely spaced buildings of the **open air museum** come into view. Go over the old railway bridge to reach the village beside the Post Office. Cross into a narrow lane and at the Fox and Hounds turn right to reach the church. Here a path leads between houses into an open field which extends to a road at Charlton. Cross and follow the lane opposite around to the Fox Inn.

Now follow the road back towards Singleton. Beyond the cross-roads a path, to the right, ascends to the Nature Reserve at **Levin Down**. In the Reserve, take the right-hand path which traverses around the hillside and continue downhill to join a bridleway beside an expired quarry. Go uphill for 60 yards to reach a plethora of choices. Take the right-hand path (which heads almost due north) descending to a heavily rutted section, beyond which it enters trees to commence a long uphill haul to Heyshott Down.

Cross a wide gravelled track, bear right, then turn left into a short dark stretch of path to reach the South Downs Way. Turn left along the Way for one more mile to return to the start. On a clear day the humps of the Isle of Wight are visible from this final section of the walk, as is the outward climb which shows prominently, snaking up the hill from the car park.

POINTS OF INTEREST:

Singleton – This downland village of flint cottages and narrow twisting lanes is situated on the old turnpike road that ran from the Surrey border to Chichester. The building housing the local shop and Post Office was originally the toll house for this stretch of road.

Open Air Museum – The Weald and Downland Open Air Museum occupies a 40 acre site on the outskirts of Singleton. It contains over 35 historic buildings rescued from various sites in southern England, restored and re-erected on site. During the summer months regular 'special days' are held, all relating to differing country activities.

Levin Down – The Down is owned by the Goodwood Estate but leased to the Sussex Wildlife Trust who manage it as a downland Site of Special Scientific Interest. It is a remnant of the ancient downland turf that once clothed much of the South Downs. Famous for its juniper bushes and colonies of orchids, it also houses many other chalk loving plants and shrubs.

REFRESHMENTS:
The Fox Inn, Charlton.

Walk 80   **St Leonard's Forest**   9m (14¹/₂km)
Maps: OS Sheets Landranger 187; Pathfinder 1246, 1247 and 1268.
A moderately strenuous walk around remnants of this ancient Wealden Wood.
Start: At 194314, the Leechpool Wood car park.

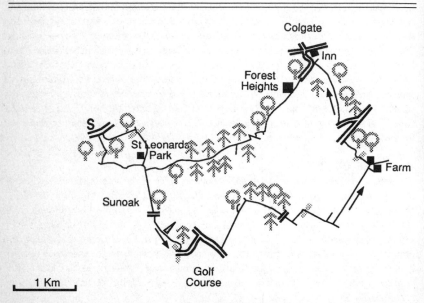

The footpath passes to the right of the car park: follow it down to a footbridge. Cross and turn alongside, or maybe in, a wet gully. Turn left along the access road to St Leonard's Place. Where the drive bends towards the house, go right through a gate and walk along a wide, straight track that crosses a lane beside the **Sunoak**. Drop down to the head of a pond and, on emerging from the wood, ignore the stile on the left, snaking away to join a road beside Golding's Bridge. Turn left and walk up to a T-junction. Turn right. The road edges a golf course: turn left into a belt of trees and at a fork continue along a muddy bridleway. Where the conifers begin, turn right (unsignposted) down their edge (or in the field) to reach a wide farm bridge. Cross and go back into the pines. Cross a lane and continue, then turn left across a field to a

154

non-existent bridge over Newstead Gill. If the stream is in flood, an easier crossing is just a few yards to the right. Once over climb the ridge. Ignore the footpath, turning left on the farm drive. At the buildings, drop left to the stream, then climb an overgrown path to reach a road. Go right for 600 yards, then turn sharp left into Woodlands Lane.

Take a path on the right which veers across a field and continue on a track through a wood. Cross a wet section beside ponds and climb again to a road. Turn right for the Dragon Inn, Colgate. After a stop, retrace your steps to follow the drive past the farm and Forest Heights. Almost level, the track continues along the edge of a section of **St Leonard's Forest** before sloping down towards a stud farm. Break right beside a stream and at the next junction turn right, then left and finally right again into conifers. Now wander between mature plantations and new plantings, maintaining a direct line and ignoring any side paths. Leave the Forestry Commission woods close to a motorcycle grass track and cross into a derelict wood. One final field is crossed before rejoining the outward route. The outward route can be retraced, but better is to use the drive to St Leonards Park which is a public right of way, even though the painted signs disagree. Turn half-left beside the last house into a narrow path and follow it down to a footbridge. Cross and re-enter Leechpool Wood. At the signpost leave the footpath by turning left beside an old barbed wire fence following a path around to the starting car park.

POINTS OF INTEREST:
Sunoak – The Sunoak is the local equivalent of the Irish Dungarven Oak, so remember to doff your hat as you pass. This specimen is over 350 years old and is protected by preservation orders. Once Morris Men performed a ritual dance around its trunk at a summer festival, possibly on Midsummer's Eve. Now forsaken, the tree is being attacked by honey fungus, but hopefully it should stand for a few years yet.

St Leonard's Forest – The forest is now very fragmented and has many plantations of alien species. It was home to one of Sussex's most famous legends – that of a serpent or dragon nine feet long. This beast, usually sighted close to the settlements of Faygate or Colgate, did not attack humans but left behind a snail-like residue which had an obnoxious smell and was poisonous. The forest's patron, St Leonard, tried on several occasions to kill the beast – where the Saints blood spilled on to the forest floor, clumps of Lily of the Valley grew and flourished.

REFRESHMENTS:
The Dragon Inn, Colgate.

Walk 81　　　DUNCTON　　　9m (14½km)

Maps: OS Sheets Landranger 197; Pathfinder 1266 and 1286.
A visit to an inn with an English tradition.
Start: At 976215, Petworth town car park.

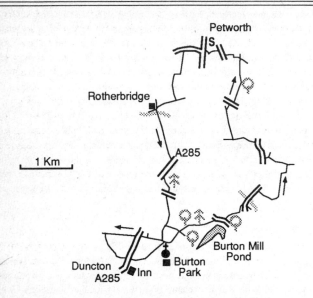

Leave the car park at its lower end and on to the Midhurst road. Just past a gatehouse a path leads through fields towards the Downs. Turn right at the cottages. At Rotherbridge the old turnpike joins from the right: cross the river and follow this track to reach the A285 at an old railway bridge. The abandoned station is still recognizable across the road. Cross, with care, and follow an uphill path. Prior to a garage, turn left into an enclosed bridleway. Follow this to a road. Cross and follow a farm road through cultivated parkland. At the buildings turn right to reach the church and the main road. Cross to a path which squeezes between two white cottages. Do not cross the field: instead, work along the headland towards Ridlington Farm, but before reaching the buildings turn left beside an overgrown stream following this path back to the village via the local school. The return path is opposite – along the driveway of St Michael's – but turn right for the **Cricketers Inn**, about 200 yards away.

Return to St Michael's entrance. At the end of the trees bear half-left over grass to reach a familiar path junction. Spare a few minutes to visit the tiny **church**, then continue along the tarmac beside the modern buildings. Where this drive turns away, enter woodland on an excellent path to **Burton Mill**. Beside the sluice another path goes through a small wood before following a field edge – you may feel inclined to use the old line across to a stile. Go left to cross both the old railway and river bridges before, in order to reduce road walking, turning right for a detour by way of Bigenor Farm. Note the old Victorian letterbox built into the wall beside the cottages. A left turn at a crossing path leads back to the road. Turn right, and, at a sharp bend, go left to follow the stream across fields to pass between a house and barn. After the next right turn, as you cross the field, the tower of Petworth Church becomes fleetingly visible. Break away from an access track to a road. Cross and walk in front of Haslingbourne then follow footprints over the field of an unsocial farm. Keep to the left of the trees before climbing over a knoll. The valley below is one option for the proposed town bypass, the other being a tunnel or cutting through Petworth park – result, long term stalemate.

Turn left along garden fences and right at a road. A narrow path, left, at the surgery now leads through county council housing before rounding a tiny green to return to the car park.

POINTS OF INTEREST:

The Cricketers Inn – The inn is on the site of a 16th-century brewery and was known as the Swan until 1867 when it was bought by John Wisden of almanac fame. Two famous Sussex cricketers were born in Duncton: James Broadridge who, in 1820, introduced overarm bowling; and James Dean, the king of 'roundarm'. The inn sign has Dean, who died inside in 1881, and W G Grace.

Church – The tiny church of St Michael contains several interesting items. Painted on the south wall is the royal coat of arms of King Charles II, dated 1636. Across the nave is a 16th-century painting of St Wilgefortis – depicted upside-down with her red hair flowing free. The brass tablet showing Lady Elizabeth Goulding wearing a heraldic tabard is the only one in England of a lady wearing this male form of dress.

Burton Mill – It is built on the site of an ancient forge which operated from Tudor times until the early 18th century, the mill pond being the original hammer pond. The site is now a Site of Special Scientific Interest owned by the Sussex Wildlife Trust.

REFRESHMENTS:
The Cricketers Inn, Duncton.
Plenty of opportunities in Petworth.

Walk 82 WARNINGLID 9m (14½km)

Maps: OS Sheets Landranger 198; Pathfinder 1268.
An up and down walk to a showcase village.
Start: At 214225, Cowfold recreation ground car park.

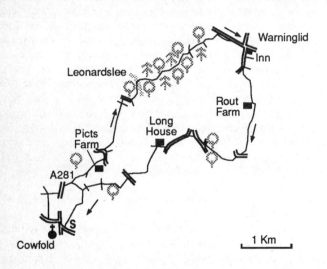

Return to the village centre and follow the road opposite the Coach House, the A272. Take the footpath to the right, by Thorndon, going over a small rise. Turn right to follow a stream to A281. Cross, with care, and go left to reach the drive to Littlebrook, on the right. Go left beside a line of oaks to a new footbridge, beyond which a path climbs out of the valley to pass Picts Farm. At a lane continue uphill then drop steeply. Take a track on the right which misses a house before turning, beside an old shed, half-left to cross to the right of a tile-roofed cottage. A wide fenced path now climbs steadily. There is a staggered junction, but keep to the main track to reach a road.

Turn right along the road, then left, beside the nurseries, on to a bridleway. There now follows nearly 2 miles of woodland walking: drop down to cross the ponds at the edge of the **Leonardslee Estate**, then climb up a gully and at a slab bridge bear left to climb slowly above the stream. Pass a modern hammer pond, ignore the side paths and when almost at civilisation, dip left into the hanger. Climb out and keep to the path as it parallels the road. On joining the road the Half Moon Inn and **Warninglid** is just over the brow.

From the inn, go left along The Street. As the road turns at the Rifleman, keep ahead on the farm drive. Turn left into the yard at Rout Farm, then go right to begin a descent through fields and orchards. As you fall there are extensive views to the downs. Join a farm track for the last few yards to a road. Go right for 50 yards to a path, left, that drops to a stream, then rises to woodland and a private drive. Go straight over to the Slaugham road. A short cut-off path on the left traverses gardens to reach another lane. Walk ahead, then turn right into a field beside the entrance to Long House. Skirt the house and, beside the pond, drop into another belt of woodland.

The path keeps to the edge of the grounds of Wellhurst Manor: at the road cross and skip left to a kissing gate. Cross the field beyond, but do not enter the wood: instead, turn right along its edge to continue on a wide grassy headland. Ignore a crossing path, then at the second stile on the right, beside an oak, go through a swampy area to reach a narrow footbridge. Cross and go diagonally over a field to reach a path that wanders back to the sports field.

POINTS OF INTEREST:

Leonardslee Estate – The walk just clips the boundary fence of Leonardslee Gardens which are one of the largest and most spectacular woodland gardens in England. The entrance to this 240 acre extravaganza is 2 miles north of Cowfold. Open throughout the summer months, the recommended times for visiting are late spring (May) for the display of azaleas and rhododendrons and October for Autumn's colours. Semi-wild families of wallabies live in the gardens, the high wire fence ensuring they do not go visiting.

Warninglid – At one time the village businesses underwent a session of musical chairs. The licence from the original 15th-century Half Moon Inn was transferred to the present building. As the former was also a posting house its return to a private dwelling enabled the old smithy to become the Post Office. Is that clear?

REFRESHMENTS:
The Half Moon Inn, Warninglid.

Walks 83 & 84   COBDEN CIRCULARS   9m (14½km) or 10m (16km)

Maps: OS Sheets Landranger 197; Pathfinder 1266 and 1286.

A reasonably level walk round settlements connected with a 19th-century statesman.

Start: At 885213, Grange Road car park, Midhurst.

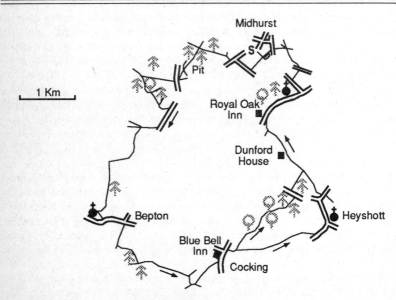

Leave from the bottom of the car park, cross a footbridge and turn right. Follow a path below the houses to a road and turn right past the fire station. At the bend, cross, left, towards the industrial estate and immediately go into trees, then follow a power-line ride between pines. Turn left on a cross path, then leave the pit edge to step right on to a parallel path. Cross a narrow road and bear right among conifers. The first section of the path is surfaced with rejects of the local 'Midhurst Whites' bricks. Fork left to temporarily join a track, then circle a garden, and cross an old railway trackbed and a field to reach a drive. Go left to a road and turn towards the Downs.

Take the road used as a public path opposite the Cowdray-coloured Lane End Cottage then, at a junction, turn sharp left along headlands. Beyond a tree-shrouded cottage go over a stile on to an access track which leads to a farm, church and duckpond. At the road, go left and walk to a T-junction. Turn right on a path which goes through trees and climbs steadily to a junction. Turn left and descend gently. Fork right at the next junction, then keep left around a well-hidden residence and follow a metalled drive to the village of Cocking. The tea rooms are opposite and the Blue Bell a few yards on the left. Continue along the lane beside the Post Office, ignoring the church track and crossing in front of Stone Cottage. Squeeze right on to a concrete track and follow it to a junction where you have a choice.

The shorter route goes ahead, edging out of the trees before swinging back into woodland. The path is well signed and heads generally north-east through the trees. Turn left on a road for 150 yards, then go right along a bridleway to reach a footbridge and path junction where you rejoin the longer route.

The longer route goes up the steps and round to a barn. Now cross fields, heading initially towards a lone oak, then, beyond a crossing track, veering a little left and aiming for the centre of a wood. Beyond the trees, make for the oncoming hedge. Keep beside this, going over a hump and on to a lane. Go left to Heyshott church. Beyond Glebe Cottage, go right into damp grassland. Cross a road and go around a cricket pitch. Turn right to pass in front of cottages en-route to a barn. Cross a paddock and follow a gravel track to a path junction where you re-join the shorter walk.

Walk past Dunford House and into a sunken drive. At the top of a rise, in front of the **Cobden obelisk,** leave the tarmac, going right, through parkland, to meet a road at the rear of the Royal Oak. Go right for 800 yards, then turn left into Church Road. Go past the school and church, then go right, through High Standing Lane. Cross right to go behind the stables, then follow field edges down to Wharf Bridge. A left turn now takes you back to the start.

POINTS OF INTEREST:

Cobden obelisk – Cocking and Heyshott share a famous son. Richard Cobden was born at Dunford Farm in 1804 and during his early years regularly worshipped at Heyshott Church. He then moved to Manchester and became MP for Stockport. He was a staunch believer in free trade and was leader of the anti-Corn Law League. The League finally succeeded in its aims in 1846. Cobden is buried in the family grave at West Lavington.

REFRESHMENTS:
The Blue Bell, Cocking.
The Royal Oak, Midhurst (on the route).

Walk 85   **KINGSMILL**   9¹/₂m (15km)

Maps: OS Sheets Landranger 198; Pathfinder 1267.

A visit to Hillaire Belloc's village and an unusual inn.

Start: At 184225, the car park beside the Little Chef on the A272.

From the lower section of this County Council car park walk past the platforms of the old station, go through the arch and follow the Downs Link trail south. The track is at first enclosed in a tree-lined cutting, but soon widens. An iron gate, across the track, directs you to a path on the right which drops to a road. Go right for 100 yards, then left at a signpost to cross fields to West Grinstead church. Enter the churchyard, turn right along a path and through a small iron gate. Go left along a path to reach the A24. Cross with care and follow a metalled bridleway through Knepp Park. Pass a pond and continue until Knepp Castle comes into view. The path now leaves the drive and, unsigned, goes through a white gate on the left. Cross grassland towards a junction of gravelled drives and turn left, then left again beside an overgrown bridge. Cross more grassland and pass a clump of three oaks to reach a belt of trees and a road. Cross, and

162

follow the path opposite to the edge of Shipley. Follow the road through the houses to **Kingsmill**. The path opposite bypasses Church Farm to reach a junction. Go left to reach a lane and then straight ahead to a T-junction. Go left for 70 yards, then right along a driveway. Go through an area of equestrian activities and turn north along a fenced track to the road at Broomfield Barn. Go left, with care, and after 100 yards take the path on the right. Follow this through fields, ignoring all paths to the left, to reach the **George and Dragon Inn**.

Now take the road signposted to West Grinstead. Pass a junction and timber-framed Well Cottage to reach, on a right-hand bend, a bridleway to the left. This becomes a footpath, then passes a cottage to reach a road beneath power lines. Cross and follow a path that crosses a stream and becomes a farm track. Go past Old Keepers Cottage and, on a sharp left bend, walk ahead to woodland and a dual section of the A24. Cross the first section, with care, and turn right along the verge of the second to reach the Copsale road. Almost immediately, beside Bar Cottage, force a way into an overgrown, enclosed path, following it to a rutted farm track. Follow the track to rejoin the Downs Link, ignoring side paths going under power lines again. Turn right for an easy amble back to the start.

POINTS OF INTEREST:

Kingsmill – This was the last (1879) and largest smock mill built in Sussex. A smockmill differs from a tower mill by having its upper floors built from wood not brick. Hillaire Belloc moved here in 1906, acquiring 'Kingsland' adjacent to the mill. The mill continued working till 1926, but until his death in 1953 Belloc kept a watchful eye on his 'baby'. Subsequently a trust was set up to renovate and restore the mill. It is open to the public infrequently in the summer.

The George and Dragon Inn – The garden has a memorial cross to a young albino who committed suicide after being wrongly accused of a petty theft. Disputes with the local clergy led to the removal of the cross from Shipley churchyard to its present home. The landlord has the full account of the tragic incident.

REFRESHMENTS:

The George and Dragon Inn, Dragons Green.
The Little Chef, West Grinstead.

Walk 86   **RUDGWICK**   9$\frac{1}{2}$m (15km)

Maps: OS Sheets Landranger 187; Pathfinder 1246.

A visit to an unspoilt Sussex pub using portions of two designated ways.

Start: At 091343, the Kings Head Inn, Rudgwick. Roadside parking is available 400 yards below the pub.

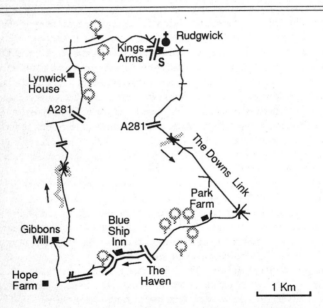

Beside the Inn a Sussex Border Path signpost points into the churchyard. Follow this designated path through fields to a junction of five ways. Turn right along a lane. This bridleway diverts left to avoid a dwelling, then continues on to a pleasant track (Bowcroft Lane). Cross the A281 with care and stroll along the Downs Link bridleway opposite for 1$\frac{1}{2}$ miles. Cross the River Arun and an isolated seat (with a view to nowhere) and, immediately after passing under a bridge, turn right up the slope of the cutting. Go through wooden gates to enter a tree lined drive, and where this turns sharply into Park Farm, cross left to reach a golf course. Follow the edge of the course down into a wood. Go over a footbridge and climb out of the ghyll. The path now inclines left, then goes along a field edge. Turn left at the next junction to reach the road among the scattering of houses that is The Haven. Turn right, and at the road junction go left along the Okehurst Road to reach the Blue Ship Inn.

Refreshed, continue towards Okehurst, and after passing Lugmore Cottage take the woodland path on the right. This crosses a ride, re-enters the trees and finally reaches a road opposite Heathers Farm. Turn right and, on a bend, go ahead along the drive of Hope Farm. At a crossing path, turn right and sink slowly into a swampy overgrown area beside a river. Negotiate this trackless waste – nudge into the wood on your right – then cross two fields to reach Gibbons Mill. Go right on a concrete farm track, then take the footpath beside Mill Cottage. Ignore any paths to the right to arrive at a substantial footbridge. You may encounter miniature horses grazing in the fields: they are residents of Toy Horse International which is based at nearby Howick Farm. Cross the footbridge and climb to a road. Turn right for 80 yards, then left on to a narrow, unkept path. Emerge and cross a field towards farm buildings, but turn right along the hedgerow to the A281. Cross with care and take the path opposite which soon begins climbing beside Lynwick Hanger, with **Lynwick House** prominent to the left. On reaching a concrete track turn left and climb to the top of a rise, the effort involved being amply rewarded by the view across the southern Weald to the Downs. Turn right along the Border Path and follow this for $1\frac{1}{2}$ miles to a road. Turn right for **Rudgwick** and the Kings Head.

POINTS OF INTEREST:

Lynwick House – In the early years of this century, the house was owned by a German advocate of community care. He loved both his estate and Rudgwick, and each Saturday sent two of his workmen around the village to tidy up and bury any litter. During the 1914-18 war, because of his nationality, he was placed under virtual house arrest. Shortly after peace came he sold up and moved away.

Rudgwick – The village was once known as the place where they sold fat pigs, one monster of the local breed being reported to have tipped the scales at 1624lbs. Parts of the village church are early 14th century. The Kings Head Inn accommodated the labourers when the church was undergoing a rebuild. Rumour has it that a secret passage between the church and cellars of the pub enabling the workers to return unseen for a 'quick one'.

REFRESHMENTS:
The Kings Head, Rudgwick.
The Blue Ship, The Haven.

Maps: OS Sheets Landranger 197; Pathfinder 1304 and 1305.
A level walk around different areas of the Manhood Peninsula.
Start: At 770980, the pay car park by East Head.

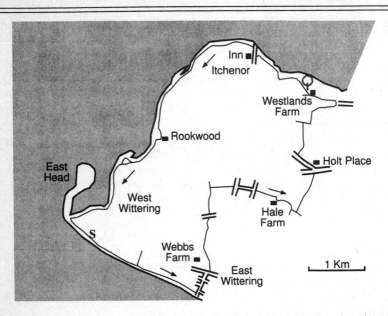

Go through a convenient gap on to the sea shore and turn left for a bracing 1¹/₂ mile walk to East Wittering, beside beaches that are the best in West Sussex. The two Witterings are kept apart by one field spared from development and extending right up to the shingle. At a bar across the path, beside a white house, turn left into an alley and road. Follow Jolliffe Road to its beginning, then go right, and very shortly left, along a footpath at the side of a caravan park. Follow the path along the side of the field to a signpost, conveniently showing against the trees. Continue through scrub to a road. Cross, go right and very soon left on a path by a metal post. Go over a footbridge and bear right across a field to a belt of trees and a road junction. Do not change direction, following the road to another T-junction where a rough path (with accompanying ditch) heads towards Hale Farm. Go around the buildings and follow the path across the neck of a field. Ignore a path to the right, but at a footbridge turn left to a road at Holt Place (look out for the high pitch and large expanse of thatched roofing on the roadside building). Cross into the Itchenor road, and after 500 yards turn into the caravan site.

Keep to the main road in the site and at the end bear half-left to reach a cross path. Turn right and walk to the entrance of Westlands Farm. The masts of anchored yachts are now appearing over the hedge. Turn left along the concrete drive, going past the farm and bearing right on a track to a copse. Go through the trees, then along a private road, turning to the waterside beside Harbour House, **Itchenor**. Sensibly the path turns inland, by the sailing club building, to reach the Ship Inn. From the inn walk down to the hard and beside the Harbour Conservancy Office turn left on to a shore line path. On certain sections, at low tide, it is possible to walk along the edge of the saltmarsh. Approaching Rookwood, where the path turns inland around houses, Hayling Island and East Head come into view. Beyond Lane End, if the tide permits, a side path allows a diversion by the spit of Ella Nore. Keep to the water's edge across the open green at Snow Hill, from where it is a short step back to the start near **East Head**.

POINTS OF INTEREST:

Itchenor – The village name derives from a Saxon tribal chief, Icca. Only ever a small settlement it was barely mentioned in the 1086 survey and has always relied heavily on the sea. A harbour for centuries, shipbuilding developed in the 17th century. Later an entrepreneur attempted to enlarge the village with an industry to rival that of Southampton. Luckily for the area, and West Sussex, the first launch was a disaster – the boat sinking. Now Itchenor is happy to be home to small craft and pleasure boating.
East Head – This sand and shingle spit extends into the entrance of Chichester Harbour. It is a mobile area, at one time projecting into the Solent. Now due to tides and weather action it has turned to face North into the harbour. It was breached in the early sixties and was in danger of being swept away. A rebuilding programme, including the planting of marram grass to stabilise the dunes, has been successful to date, but the fight goes on. The trig. pillar at the entrance is a collecting box for the National Trust which has provided waymarked paths around the Head.

REFRESHMENTS:
The Ship Inn, Itchenor.
There is a seasonal snack bar and ice creams at the car park.

Walk 88　　ARUN VALLEY WALK III　　9½m (15km)

Maps: OS Sheets Landranger 197; Pathfinder 1306.

A longer, more open stretch of the walk to the river mouth.

Start: At 024064, Arundel Station.

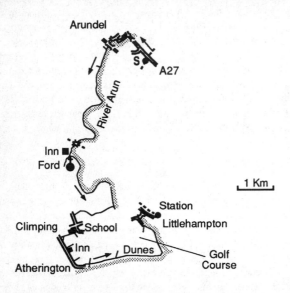

A final linear walk along the Arun Valley, with return by train.

Turn left at the end of the station approach, go straight over the roundabout and follow the old road to the river bridge. Cross, turn left and keep left of the Swan. At the entrance to Tarrant Wharf, by a tiny public garden, turn right, then left at the junction. About 20 yards beyond Surrey Wharf a footpath back to the river is signed. On the right is Fagins Folly: have a look at the property wall – hand built and entombing many additives – false teeth, a cow's head, village pump etc. The path dips under the road then leaves the town behind. The river banks are largely artificial now, the natural bank appearing only occasionally. As you approach the sea, kelp becomes more prolific, clinging to the banks. Re-enter civilisation at **Ford** railway bridge: a cluster of boats are usually moored beside the Ship and Anchor. As you step round to the old canal two houseboats and a wreck block the entrance. A path leads across to the isolated and locked church.

After passing close to the **open prison** the river begins another long loop and passes a small sewerage works. As you approach the road bridge, slant away to a gate, then drop right to a footbridge. In the field beyond, the right of way crosses direct to the corner of the caravan park, but the path is little used and the farmer unco-operative: if crops bar your progress take the long way around the field. Go over a ditch then cross towards the church. Follow a hedgerow to a road. Turn left, go straight over the roundabout and turn right to the school. Follow a tarmac cross-field path and bear left into a twitten, following it to **Climping** village street. The yellow lines confirm that this is a very busy lane in summer. Continue to the Black Horse for a well deserved break. Follow the lane past the **Bailiffscourt Hotel** before ending abruptly at the shingle. Go through the left-hand car park to join the shoreline path. The footpath turns away from the shore but a consolidated shingle way extends along the edge of the dunes to the breakwater where you have to go inland. Seaside Littlehampton is just a few yards away over the river: stroll between the boatyards and the golf course, and at the clubhouse step right on to a metalled path that contours above the road. Walk to the marina and go right to cross the swing bridge. Turn right on Terminus Road to reach the station.

POINTS OF INTEREST:

Ford – The derivation of the name is self evident although a 12th-century spelling in the plural suggests more than one crossing. In the 19th century this tiny settlement regained some importance as the junction of the ill-fated Portsmouth Canal and the river Arun. Lock Cottage still stands beside the church.

Open prison – The prison occupies a disused World War II Fleet Air Arm airfield.

Climping – This is a single village street leading to one of the few remaining unspoilt stretches of open shoreline remaining in the county. Like Selsey, Climping has lost a neighbouring parish, Cudlow, to the encroaching sea. Try not to visit the clutter free dunes in the holiday season for they are very popular with visitors.

Bailiffscourt Hotel – This large hotel is built on the site of a former bailiff's house belonging to the chapel of a Norman abbey.

REFRESHMENTS:

The Black Horse, Climping.

There are numerous possibilities in Littlehampton.

Walk 89   **WORTH**   9½m (15km)

Maps: OS Sheets Landranger 187; Pathfinder 1247.
A heavily wooded walk close to Crawley New Town.
Start: At 323368, the Worth Way car park, Rowfant.

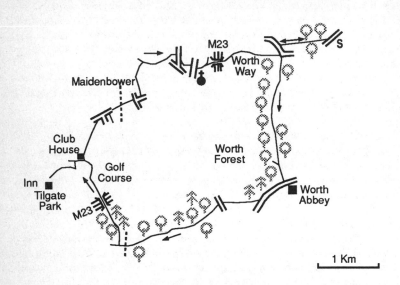

Go around a gate and follow the Worth Way westwards to a road. Turn left for 150 yards to a sharp bend, then go left over a stile beside gates. The wide estate track beyond undulates southwards through Worth Forest for nearly 1½ miles to meet a road near **Worth Abbey**. Turn right and in a gap in the rhododendrons, to the right, take a metalled drive that passes between white gates and rises over Whitely Hill. Cross a road to re-enter woodland and follow a path to a railway bridge. Go over and after 80 yards turn right between gate posts and white stumps. Cross a footbridge over the motorway, then bear half-left to the golf course in **Tilgate Park**. After crossing four fairways the path turns toward the club house: keep to the left and walk between parking areas on a yellow lined road. At a small bridge turn left beside the outflow from Tilgate Lake. Cross the head of the lake then go up the tree-covered knoll to the Inn in The Park.

Return to the club house, turn left to edge along the driving range and continue through the trees to meet the houses of Furnace Green. Turn right around a solitary tennis court and at a road go ahead past a signpost pointing back into the new town housing. Where the road ends a paved path continues under the railway to enter the recent development of Maidenbower. The rights of way appear to be retained, but small detours occur. Cross a roundabout into Maidenbower Drive and after 60 yards take a still rural path to the left, between new blocks of housing. Cross a road and keep right in the trees to a new footbridge over the Gatwick Stream. Go right on a tarmac path to reach the Worth Way. Turn right. At the next bridge follow signs up steps to the road and at the roundabout cross into the drive to Stone Court. Go behind houses, cross into Church Lane and then veer left a few yards before the **church**. Recross the motorway and go through a farm to follow a track to the corner where you first entered the forest. Now reverse the outward route to the start.

POINTS OF INTEREST:

Worth Abbey – The mock Tudor mansion of Paddockhurst was built in 1870 and owned by Sir Robert Whitefield, the inventor of the torpedo. One of the few persons to gain financially from their brainchild he utilised the garden pool for his experiments. The next owner, who became the first Lord Cowdray, extended both the house and estate. After his death it was acquired by Downside and converted into a boys public school. A monastery was added and the name was changed to Worth Abbey.

Tilgate Park – The Park is the main lung of the Crawley New Town development. Although on the edge of the housing, it has been designed to give an immediate entry into a tranquil atmosphere, apart from the unavoidable M23 traffic roar. Beyond the centre complex is the nature centre – usually the first stop for the children.

Church – At one time Worth claimed to be, geographically, the largest parish in England. As increased development occurred new parishes were formed from the mater. The Saxon church is an enigma – when was it built and why is it so large? – since the area was only a clearing in the great Anderida Forest. In 1986 during treatment of the roof timbers, a fire broke out. Luckily only the roof was destroyed; but it gave an opportunity for more thorough restoration.

REFRESHMENTS:
The Inn in The Park, Tilgate Park.

Maps: OS Sheets Landranger 197 and 198; Pathfinder 1267.
A walk on lesser used paths east of Billingshurst.
Start: At 086260, the library car park, Billingshurst.

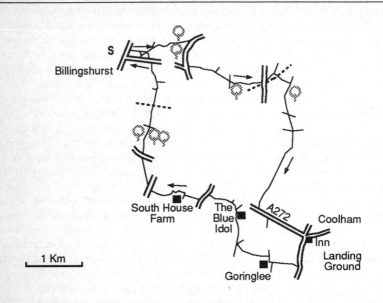

Take the one-way road to the village centre and turn left to cross at the pelican. Walk
to the end of the shops and turn into Little East Street. At the last bungalow go ahead
into an area known locally as 'The Bowling Alley'. Emerge from blackthorn and
cross to a field corner. Pass beneath power lines into a copse. At the lane turn right
and, a few yards before it joins a road, go left to follow a fence. Where it turns away,
go half-right to a step over wire. Cross a field to a footbridge, continuing to a double
gate. Keep ahead beside a line of young oaks, then go left over a ditch and climb a
flight of steps to a road adjacent to a railway bridge. Squeeze between the railway and
an extended garden, then follow a drive, going right over a bridge and passing Hook
Farm. When the drive bends left, go right on a bridleway. Change sides of the hedge
at a drinking trough, go under power lines and veer half-left to a gate to a track. Do

not take the footpath: instead, go left and, as the track turns towards a farm, go right through a gate. Zig-zag left and right, and follow a bridleway to the A272.

Cross, with care, and turn left to reach the Selsey Arms. From the inn, take the Storrington road, passing the **Coolham airstrip**, and, opposite Farleys Cottage, go right on a footpath. At Goringlee, go right between the old and modern barns, then left to keep above a small stream. Go right to a corner stile and the next farm. Go right, along the access track and, a few yards beyond a gate, you arrive at the **Blue Idol**. Continue for a few yards to reach a fenced path to the left. Go around a burial ground, cross a field and then climb beside an old farmhouse to a road. Turn left for 200 yards, then go right through a donkey paddock. Keep to the right of South House Farm, follow the drive and, at the nursery entrance, bear left and almost immediately swing right along a hedgerow. At a road, turn right for 100 yards, then go left along a drive. After a few steps go right past a stable block. Negotiate a garden to rejoin the road. Cross right into Kingsfold. Follow a path through a copse, past rear gardens and through an industrial estate before crossing the railway. Now follow a farm drive to the Billingshurst boundary. Turn left and drop down to the village centre.

POINTS OF INTEREST:

Coolham airstrip – The Coolham advanced landing ground (ALG) had a short operational life of a little over three months. It was built with two runways in 1943, but was leased as grazing until the first squadrons arrived in April 1944. The multi-national crews departed for Funtington ALG on 4 July. A lone, and last, visitor was a damaged Liberator bomber in January 1945. A memorial to those who never returned stands in the garden of the Selsey Arms.

Blue Idol – The origin of the name of this yeoman farmhouse is unknown. It was adapted by the Quakers into a meeting house and William Penn, when living at Warminghurst was, along with his family, a regular worshipper. His daughter, Letitia, is buried in the nearby graveyard. Today the building is not only a place of worship, but a guest house.

REFRESHMENTS:

The Selsey Arms, Coolham.
There are several possibilities in Billingshurst.

Walk 91   **FOUR COUNTIES**   10m (16km)

Maps: OS Sheets Landranger 187; Pathfinder 1248 and 1228.

A walk from East Grinstead into three neighbouring counties.

Start: At 403397, Woodlands Road, at the eastern edge of the town.

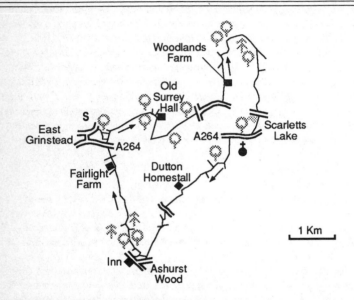

Go to the end of the road, downhill and 50 yards beyond the end of the footway cross into a wood. Follow arrows to the edge of the wood and turn left, keeping close to the trees. At the next junction, go diagonally across a field to a gate. Maintain direction to join a track through the trees. Fork right in front of Old Surrey Hall and go down the drive. Before the next buildings break left: the path skirts a wood then drops left to a footbridge. Turn right over a horse jump, keep above Kent Water and go through a belt of trees to reach a waymarked gate. Go left at a lane, turn right at a junction and, after about 600 yards, turn left on a bridleway. Pass Woodlands Farm and climb towards Dry Hill. Go around the buildings of the next farm then, beside a pond, go right. Where the path jinks you cross into Kent. Fork right at the junction in the wood. Leave, then re-enter the trees to continue on a path. Next, keep to field edges to join a track beside a pond. Follow the track off the ridge, cross a lane and, past Scarletts Lake, enter East Sussex. At the A264, go right, with care, passing a church and the entrance to Hammerwood to turn left at a white bungalow.

At the end of an enclosed section of path, veer half-right to a wood corner. Keep to the tree edge and go ahead on a drive. Go left around Brooklands, then over a stile into a field. Follow a track through **Homestall Stud**. Cross a lane and drop between gate posts. Climb to a school and go over a stile, right, back into West Sussex. Veer half-left to a gate, keep left to reach a track that, beyond a farm, becomes a drive. At a road turn half-right for the Three Crowns. Cross back left into Ivy Dene Lane. Bear left at the industrial complex, then right through a garden gate: the path crosses the lawn and rises into trees between outcrops of rocks. Go along the edge of the wood. After a path joins, continue beside a newly planted area. Go right at a junction, then left to a stile. Now follow a path to Fairlight Farm, prominent across the valley, taking care not miss the first plank bridge. Turn right along the drive to reach the A264. Go left for 30 yards then cross, with care, to a Border Path sign pointing in to an area used for tipping. Turn left, then follow a line of furze to join the outward path back to the start.

POINTS OF INTEREST:

Homestall Stud – Homestall House was originally a hunting lodge owned by John of Gaunt. Massive reconstruction took place in 1933 – Dutton Hall was transported from Cheshire and added, giving an alien West Midland timber frame to the Sussex landscape. In celebration the name was hyphenated to Dutton Homestall.

This walk encounters typical waymarks of the four county authorities. The West Sussex finger posts are familiar to users of this book. Surrey uses plastic arrows for its inter-road paths, but sparingly. Kent is a little more generous and their marks also contain the path numbers, where required. East Sussex are now using a smarter arrow, but are still reluctant to publicise all of their off road departure points.

REFRESHMENTS:
The Three Crowns, Ashurst Wood.
There are also numerous possibilities in East Grinstead.

Walk 92   **THE BEDHAM HILLS**   10m (16km)
Maps: OS sheets Landranger 197; Pathfinder 1267 and 1287.
A fine crossing of these wooded hills.
Start: At 024237, the Mens car park, Crimbourne Lane.

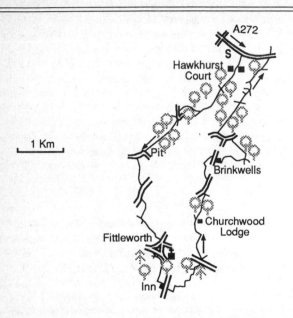

Turn right from the car park, then go along the drive to **Hawkhurst Court**. Take the right fork between the buildings, then, beyond the pond, drop to a bridge. Leave the drive to the right along a bridleway into beech woods with holly underscrub. Go straight over a crossing path and past an information board to walk between some isolated Bedham properties. Follow the hoof prints to the right, back into trees, ignoring a left fork to follow a power line before swinging up to a lane. Go uphill to a U-bend and there select the centre path of the three on the right. Drop gently past a quarry to reach a narrow road. Go right and round a bend and, at the end of River Hill Lodge gardens, go left into a field. Head for three oaks, then follow telegraph poles to a stile on to a road: the water garden opposite is worth a moment's admiration. Turn right, then left towards the orchards. After a few yards, go right along a field edge to a footbridge. Cross and keep beside the stream to a path junction. Turn left through a field, heading towards a clump of beech trees. Now roughly follow a garden hedge to a pair of gates on to a road.

Go right, to a T-junction and use the slip road past the church. Cross the next road, and at the end of the white cottages turn left through a birch wood to a gravelled drive. This swings left to the Swan Inn. From the inn, cross right on to a track below a farm. Go over a stile, left, and along headlands to a drive. Go right for 50 yards, then climb to a common. A right fork takes you down to the main road (the A283). Cross, with care, and turn left to an iron gate (on the right). Keep to the left-hand path through a chestnut copse, then go ahead along a strip of tarmac. This swings left and ends at Churchwood Lodge. Climb up through chestnuts, then turn left to reach a road. Turn right, uphill, then go left on a footpath. The right of way swings away from the old track before re-discovering the underfoot evidence. At a road retreat downhill (right) to the access for **Brinkwells**, to the left. Pass the cottage, with its plaque, and go left into trees. Contour below a nettled bank to a farm entrance. Keep to the edge of the wood before striking half-left across to a field corner. Drop left, then turn left to collect a house drive. At the road, turn left to a T-junction. Take the Petworth road almost to the brow: after the 1987 storm, this road was rendered traffic free for over three weeks. Turn right and start a long, straight descent back through the Bedham Woods. After a horse barrier, edge out of the trees, squeeze past paddocks and slither into a ghyll. Scramble out to join a metalled track serving scattered properties. The next path can easily be missed: it goes left on a bend, where another drive departs right. It is also ill-defined in places: aim to close on the right-hand wood edge and continue to a road (Crimbourne Lane). Turn left to return to the start.

POINTS OF INTEREST:

Hawkhurst Court – This was once a school, but is now a block of luxury apartments. During World War II it was home to Canadian forces and from here the disastrous 1942 Dieppe raid was planned and 'executed'. Each year a memorial service is held in Wisborough Green church.

Brinkwells – In the early years of this century, this was home to a group of artists, whose watering hole was the Swan Inn at Fittleworth. During the summers of 1917-21, the composer Edward Elgar made his base here, composing his cello concerto and a selection of chamber music.

REFRESHMENTS:
The Swan Inn, Lower Fittleworth.

Walk 93   BALCOMBE AND WEST HOATHLY   10½m (17km)

Maps: OS Sheets Landranger 187; Pathfinder 1247.

Cross and recross the sandstone ridges north-east of Balcombe.

Start: At 307309, Balcombe Church.

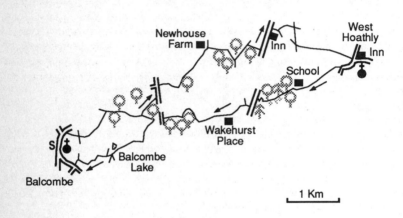

Walk away from the village and at the bottom of the slope, go right through the gates on to a road. Pass a pond and walk to a stone bridge. About 50 yards into a wood fork right, cross duck boards and climb through fields: Worth Abbey is on the left skyline. Turn left into the next wood to meet a lane to the right of two cottages. Go left and, at a road junction, go right along Newhouse Farm drive. Go past a hammer pond and climb beside a small stream. Cross, right, in front of farm cottages and go over a ridge. Clamber down through trees to a footbridge. At the junction beyond, turn left up a path/rocky stream bed: there is little improvement until a farm is reached. At a road, turn left to the White Hart Inn. Just beyond, to the right, you rejoin the Gravetye walk. Drop down to a bridge and enter a field keeping beside the rhododendrons. Ignore a gap in the fence and obliquely cross a drive to a stile at the rear of a house.

Turn right on the crossing path towards a farm. Go through kissing gates, then go left on along a drive and through fields to West Hoathly and the Cat Inn.

Walk down The Street, passing the **Priest House,** and at a right-angled bend keep ahead on an unmade drive to four 'Philpotts'. Beyond the school, turn right and descend a bulldozed track. An estate path winds along the valley floor beside small ponds: at a T-junction go right and climb a rocky zig-zag to a road. Turn left for 300 yards to the entrance to **Wakehurst Place,** to the right. Follow the drive round to a high brick wall, then go down between deer fences. Cross the neck of the National Trust gardens to a pair of footbridges and start climbing again. Keep left in the field to reach a lane. Cross to a farm drive, go into a field and follow the hedge before slanting away to a gate at the corner of a wood. Turn right to join a concrete track on its way to Balcombe Lake. Cross a stile at the end of the water and go half-left to a signpost on the skyline (beside the right-hand oak of four). Turn left, then right over the cricket ground to reach a fenced path. Follow it back to the village. At the shops go right, then right again to reach the start.

POINTS OF INTEREST:

Priest House – This house in West Hoathly is a 15th-century wattle and daub timberframe operated by the Sussex Archaeological Society as a domestic museum. First owned by the Clunic monks of Lewes, it was a recruitment centre for Jack Cade's abortive rebellion against Henry VI. The monks let the house to the Browne family who remained tenants even after the Dissolution of the Monasteries. They finally bought the property from Queen Elizabeth I.

Wakehurst Place – The house was built in 1590 by a descendant of the long-established Culpepper family, though it was in the early years of this century when Gerald Loder, brother of Sir Edmund of Leonardslee, began to transform the estate by establishing a collection of rare specimen trees and flowering shrubs. The gardens are leased to the Royal Botanic Society, the 520 acres being world famous and known as 'Kew in the County'.

REFRESHMENTS:
The Cat Inn, West Hoathly.
The Half Moon, Balcombe.

Walk 94   RACTON AND NUTBOURNE   10½m (17km)

Maps: OS Sheets Landranger 197; Pathfinder 1304.
Above and beside the sea in the south-west corner of the County.
Star: At 755073, Westbourne church.

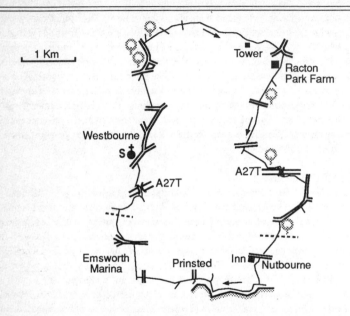

From the church, go past the shops to The Square and take the left fork. Turn right into River Street. Go past the old mill building and accompany its elongated pond to a T-junction. Cross a bridge and go right at the end of the first terrace. Now, beside the pigeon lofts, slide into fields. Follow the stiles up to a road junction. Maintain direction (the signpost says Stanstead House), then go right on a bridleway. After 100 yards, fork right and walk along an easily graded track for well over a mile. After passing the ruined **Racton Tower** you ease gently down to another road junction. The entry to Racton Park Farm is a few yards up the Chichester road: at the end of this concrete drive continue to a wood. Take the right fork and walk to a road.

    Cross the road to a fenced path and follow it down past a farm to the Woodmancote Arms. Pass to the right of the inn, then swing left behind the houses. Follow a path across a field and go right for a bridge over the **A27T**. Once clear of this pseudo-motorway, bear left and pass a series of watercress beds to reach a road. Turn right, and right again at a junction. Just prior to the fish farm, go left over several new stiles and plank bridges. Squeeze between a wood and a pond, cross a railway and follow field edges to Nutbourne: a few doors beyond the Bell and Anchor there is a Little Chef.

Leave Farm Lane by the NRA sign and follow a well-trodden path to the sea wall. Turn right. On reaching the road end at Prinsted, leave the wall and strike inland along a lane. Go to the right of Thornham House, then aim towards the masts in Emsworth marina. You catch the aroma of the sewerage works: hurriedly cross a road and an area of permanent 'set aside' to reach black and white deck houses. Turn right, continue behind all the buildings of the boat yard and go behind the houses to the road. Go left to the Royal Oak, and follow Lumley Road under the railway, and on to its end. Go through the white gates to wind around with a drive. Re-cross the A27, and, after a straight section, beside the first house, bear left beside the bourne on a metalled path that drops you opposite **Westbourne church**.

POINTS OF INTEREST:

Racton Tower – The Tower was built in 1772 for the third Earl of Halifax whose family seat was Stanstead House. Costing £10,000 to build, it was triangular in form, a large central tower surrounded by smaller towers at the corners. It was a favourite haunt of the Earl. One story relates that his lordship would invite the local excise men to review the fleet with him. Drink was freely available and when the guardians of the coast became incapable, flares were lit on the tower indicating that it was clear for contraband to come ashore.

A27T – The trunk road is not popular with local residents for the top surface emits an excessive volume of traffic noise compared with other motorways. Continued protests to the Department of Transport have had little effect, just a few cosmetic baffle walls erected in the noisiest spots.

Westbourne church – According to the guide to Westbourne church the avenue of trees leading from the north gate were planted in 1546. If this is true they probably constitute the earliest plantings in England. Certainly they are magnificent specimens.

REFRESHMENTS:
The Bell and Anchor, Nutbourne.
The Little Chef, Nutbourne.
Several inns and tea rooms in Westbourne.

Walk 95   SELSEY AND SIDLESHAM   11m (17½km)

Maps: OS Sheets Landranger 197; Pathfinder 1323.

A long, but level walk under wide open skies.

Start: At 866934, the East Beach Car Park, Selsey.

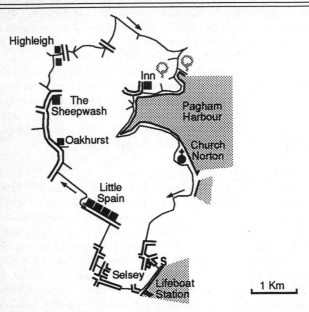

From the car park walk up on to the raised path at the edge of the shingle and turn right towards the lifeboat station. Adjacent to it is a small RNLI museum and shop. Pass under the walkway, then go inland to enter a twitten beside the Lifeboat Inn. Continue along Grove and Latham roads, turning right beside the telephone exchange into a shopping area. Cross the road and, beside the butchers, take a path between high hedges which leads to an estate road. Turn right, following the line of the **Selsey Tramway** to the golf club entrance. Turn left beside the rows of chalets in the Little Spain Country Club, then left to cross a ditch. In the next field, aim for a low grey barn to reach a metalled drive. Turn right along this for just over a mile: the Downs ahead are too distant to impose on the East Anglian type landscape. Pass a thatched barn conversion at Okehurst, and at the first bend beyond the road junction, opposite the Sheepwash, go left off the road, then turn right on a path towards Highleigh.

Cross a road and follow the path along the edge of a nursery and through fields to reach another road. The path opposite heads towards Sidlesham church: at the barns turn right along a track into open country. The path to the right is a short cut to the inn, the route continuing through poorly drained meadows to a footbridge over the Bremere Rife. Cross the next field, turning right between furze bushes to enter a scrubby wood. On reaching the sea wall keep right, beside the water, all the way to **Sidlesham Quay**. At high spring tides it will be necessary to divert inland at the next path junction, turning left when reaching the road. Walk past the mill pond and along the harbour-side track almost to a road. Now a path around the head of the creek rejoins the sea wall for its journey to Church Norton. There, go inland through the churchyard before, at a parking area, turn back to the shore. Keep as close to the fence as is comfortable, and at the end of the reed beds a path returns inland to reach a junction. Turn left on a track to the edge of the East Beech development, going via Park Farm. Go along the bungalow-lined road, and at its end, turn left past the shops to return to the car park.

POINTS OF INTEREST:

Selsey Tramway – There are very few remains of the 'Hundred of Manhood and Selsey Tramway' whose life began in 1897. It was $7^3/_4$ miles long and at no point was more than 20 feet above sea level. Very cheaply constructed, it boasted eleven stations but no signals, six level crossings but no gates. It closed finally in January 1935, another victim of road transport. To the end of it was held in affection by the local populace, many believing that the closure would only be temporary.

Sidlesham Quay – The grassy area beside the old quay was the site of an environmentally friendly tide mill. The incoming tide flowed through the mill wheel and was retained in the mill pond which is still in existence. On the ebb, water was released from the pond and again powered the wheel. When Pagham Harbour was drained in the 1870s the mill became redundant and was demolished. Pagham Harbour is a saltmarsh inlet whose entrance has regularly changed over the centuries. The entrance was closed in 1876, the marshes drained and converted into cattle grazing land. However, the sea returned in 1910. In the Second World War, prior to D-Day, the sea outside the harbour entrance was the assembly point for sections of the prefabricated Mulberry Harbours.

REFRESHMENTS:

The Lifeboat Inn, Selsey.
The Crab and Lobster, Sidlesham Quay.
There are numerous possibilities in Selsey.

Walk 96   THE HENLEY HILLS   11½m (18½km)

Maps: OS Sheets Landranger 197; Pathfinder 1266.

A heavily wooded walk across the hills to the north of Midhurst.

Start: At 895225, the priory at the eastern edge of Easebourne.

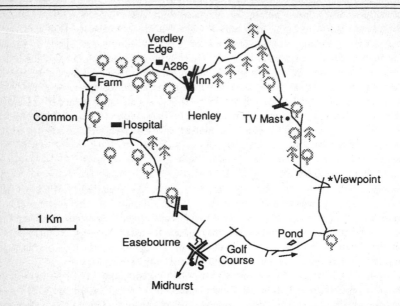

Cross the road into an old avenue of chestnut trees. Turn right on a crossing path to enter a golf course through a tall kissing gate. Follow signs across the course to a line lime trees. Skirt round Steward's Pond, **Queen Elizabeth's Oak** is behind, and follow faint tracks to a stile to exit the ancient deer park. At the wood corner, turn left on to an old road, noting the large openings of old badger sets. At the open area beyond Vining Farm, turn left and at the next farm follow the track around the head of the hanger into open woodland. Keep left at the next fork to pass the TV relay mast, then drop steeply and somewhat awkwardly to a lane. Another old road, 20 yards to the right, continues for almost a mile along the edge of Verdley Wood, finally emerging on a driveway. Almost immediately return towards the trees, but continue in the field to reach a stable before entering the conifers. Cross a stream and go along well signed forestry roads. At the first junction turn right, then left and left again at the road used as a public path (RUPP) to arrive amid the old cottages at **Henley**. The inn is a few yards uphill.

Continue uphill, then, opposite Old Henley, go right on a path up to a drive then up again to the A286. Cross, with care, to reach another old road. This track keeps below the crest, before dropping sharply to Verdley Edge. Turn back uphill, ignoring the guard dog warning and continuing to climb the main track to clear the trees. Turn right, cross a stile and break across the field to a lonely signpost and farm buildings. Go to the right of a pond and emerge on Woolbeding Common. Turn left along a track, then right through a mini parking area to reach a path that falls gently beside a bank. When back in open common, keep close to the trees and after a barren area turn left to join another footpath that soon leaves the National Trust area. The path goes below the **hospital** before beginning a steady descent through the chestnuts to reach Cherry Orchard Cottage. Follow the lane to the next house where a path swoops down to its drive and on to the main road. Cross, with care, to a gap in the barrier and go down to a white cottage. Turn right to its garage where steps lead to a field path. A right turn now brings you to the cemetery and Easebourne village.

POINTS OF INTEREST:

Queen Elizabeth's Oak – The name is given to the gnarled stump behind Steward's Pond because of a legend that Elizabeth I, whilst staying at Cowdray, shot a deer on the spot, an oak being planted to commemorate the event.

Henley – Older OS maps show a ruined castle in the woods to the north-east of Henley. Now untraceable, it had a hazy history. Was the original sacked by the Danes? Was it a Norman motted house guarding the road north from Chichester or a madhouse attached to the nunnery at Easebourne? One thing is certain, when it was demolished in 1880 the fabric and foundations were used to repair local roads.

Hospital – The King Edward VII Hospital, affectionately known as 'The Sanni', is one of the largest independent hospitals in the country. Set in 153 acres, its gardens designed by Gertrude Jekyll, it was built at the turn of the century and opened in 1906 by the King whose name it bears. For 70 years it served as a sanatorium before being converted to a modern hospital.

REFRESHMENTS:
The Duke of Cumberland, Henley.

Walk 97   **ALDINGBOURNE**   11$\frac{1}{2}$m (18$\frac{1}{2}$km)
Maps: OS Sheets Landranger 197; Pathfinder 1305.
A long, but level, walk in fields to the south-east of Chichester.
Start: At 924054, Aldingbourne Church.

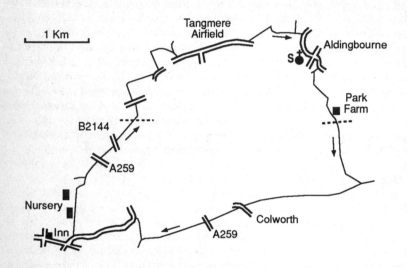

Parking is available by Aldingbourne's old vicarage.

Walk down the single track road and cross into the equally narrow Hook Lane. On the second bend, go right past a white thatched barn conversion and along the drive to Park Farm. Step into a field to skirt the last buildings and cross the railway to a farm track. Beyond the barns, go over a stile and follow a wire mesh fence surrounding a landfill site to the bank of the old canal (see Note to Walk 65). Turn right for a virtual straight walk of almost 2$\frac{1}{2}$ miles. Once clear of the tip there are extensive views to the Downs: Bignor Hill, Halnaker Windmill and the Goodwood grandstand all show clearly. Cross a large field, aiming for the end of a clump of trees 100 yards to the left of the farm buildings to rejoin the canal earthworks and nettles.

Go straight over a lane and bisect the next fields, clipping bushes, and going through an old hedge, to meet the Bognor road (the A259) at the end of a lay-by.

Cross, with care, follow field edges and cross open fields to a crossing track, where there are the remains of an old canal overbridge. Turn right to a farm. Turn left on a lane and follow it to reach a bridleway, which goes right, on a sharp bend. However, for refreshments continue along the road and go right at a junction to a roundabout and the Walnut Tree Inn, Runcton.

The walk goes along Green Lane (the bridleway), heading north beside the glasshouses. Re-cross the A259, with equal care, into the exit of Chichester Garden Centre. Opposite the last display house, step right to an enclosed path. Wind through the mobile homes and cross the B2144, left, to a centre-of-field path that leads to the railway. Continue to a road and cross to an overgrown path towards a white house: there is a good excuse here for a field edge trespass. Turn right, go left at the T-junction, then left again at the rear of a mushroom farm. A sporadic line of trees marks the edge of a byway where a right turn leads to a road junction. Here a bridleway on the left leads to the Tangmere Aviation Museum. Divert if you wish, returning to this spot to continue along the road, just outside the **airfield** boundary.

At the road end enter an old field (by the West Sussex County Council signs) and follow the taxiway, concrete that once ferried the Spitfire and Hurricane into battle in the 1940s. Beyond the first set of blast walls go right, then left and at the end of the lane Aldingbourne church beckons from the right.

POINTS OF INTEREST:

Airfield – Tangmere was one of the main fighter bases for the Battle of Britain. Its darkest hours were of 15-16 August 1940 when it was repeatedly attacked by Junkers 87 dive bombers, but somehow the station remained operational. In the later war years it became an emergency landing ground for damaged allied bombers and also housed a squadron of Lysanders who made a habit of depositing agents into occupied France. The airfield closed in 1967, but 15 years later the Military Aviation Museum was founded. Now based in four buildings, it retells the story of military flying from its earliest days, but with special emphasis on Tangmere 1939-45.

During the Battle of Britain there was no local in which the off duty pilots could relax, so they adopted the upstairs bar of the Unicorn in Chichester. In 1981 the newly built inn was named the Bader Arms in recognition of one of the stations commanders.

REFRESHMENTS:
The Walnut Tree, Runcton.

Maps: OS Sheets Landranger 197; Pathfinder 1286 and 1287.
A full day's walk over the Downs to a Roman Villa.
Start: At 002108, Whiteways Lodge car park.

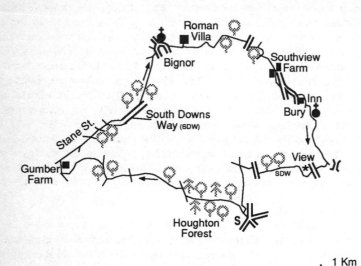

You may feel the need to stock up at the snack bar before leaving the car park as it is a fair hike to the inn.

Take the bridleway behind the iron gate into Houghton Forest, and at the bottom of the dip bear left., immediately crossing another track to regain the height lost. A bridleway joinsfrom the left and later leave the now waymarked cycleway by turning left. Mind the pheasants as you continue westwards through fields and woods. At the second bridleway, turn right, then bear left on a narrower path to **Gumber Farm** where the National Trust has converted redundant farm buildings into an upmarket bothy. Turn right through the farm, then follow Stane Street uphill. Ignore all side paths to reach a parking area and ornate signpost. Follow the arm towards Bignor and Londinium, going along a semi-metalled byway. A path then drops down to the village.

Once on the level, cross the first stile of the walk before turning right along a stream bed and going over stepping stones to a road.

Turn left and follow the road as it bears right beside the church to reach a path adjacent to a thatched cottage. Cross the drive to the **Roman Villa**, then circle a farm to leave on the access road. At the sharp bend, turn left, then right into a long belt of trees. At the road go uphill for 60 yards, then go left along a track into the wood beyond the cottages. Cross a stile and turn back along the edge of the wood. Turn left on another cross-field path to reach the corner of Southview Farm. The way through the buildings is your choice – make for the grain hopper where you drop to a gate, then go across to a stile beside a white house. Go over the road, and follow the lane in Bury to the inn where a sign proclaims 'Ramblers and walkers welcome'. Take the path beside the inn, keeping left to reach the church – the right of way runs beside the school building and enters the churchyard over a low wall. Continue to reach the River Arun at the site of the old ferry. Turn right (downstream) and follow the river bank towards the new South Downs Way bridge. Just prior to the bridge, leave the river and follow a new section of the Way to join the original trail as it starts uphill. As you climb towards the trees there are wide views towards Amberley Mount and over the river. At the road, cross, with care, turn right, then left for one final ascent. Now turn left on to a path along a field edge to reach the outward track close to the car park.

POINTS OF INTEREST:

Gumber Farm – In World War II, airfield-type lighting was installed in the fields around Gumber. In the event of a night raid this was turned on to act as a decoy for the fighter base at Tangmere. This ruse had some success as the various 'holes' in the surrounding fields are not, as thought by some, collapsed flint mine shafts; but much more recent bomb craters. At the same time as the lights, a bomb shelter was built near to the farm. It is rumoured that it may be restored as a 1940s museum.

Roman Villa – Bignor Roman Villa is one of the largest villas ever discovered in England. Built just to the west of Stane Street around 190AD it fell into decay after the departure of the Romans and was not re-discovered until 1811 when a large stone was unearthed by a local farmer during ploughing. The villa has superb mosaics, one 82 feet long, and an early underfloor central heating system. It is open to the public between March and October.

REFRESHMENTS:

The Black Dog and Duck, Bury.
The snack bar, Whiteways Lodge car park.

Maps: OS Sheets Landranger 197; Pathfinder 1285.
The Hampshire Downs and a Country Park.
Start: At 790181, the National Trust car park, Harting Down.

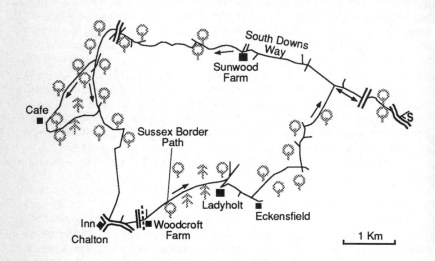

Walk across the grass to the South Downs Way (SDW) and turn left. Cross the road to descend among the trees. Go over the next road, which hosted a hill climb for the 1994 Tour de France, and follow the Way to its original end at Buriton. Cross the Sussex Border Path. Where the trees of West Harting begin a retreat, pass into Hampshire. From Sunwood Farm to the deserted buildings at Coulters Dean, the Way is metalled, while beyond North Lodge the going becomes more undulating. Walk to a road for your first encounter with the Hangers Way (HW). Go through a parking area and climb into the **Country Park**. Beyond the turning circle the walks diverge.

The shorter route follows red banded posts on a link path between the HW and the Staunton Way (SW) which joins from the right at a cross-roads. Continue towards Chalton.

The longer route goes right on a joint SDW/HW path. Descend gently, pass a barbecue area and on reaching the car park at Benham Bushes, continue down on the lower road. At civilisation, turn right to reach the information centre and café. Return to the main car park: from there follow the Staunton Way. After an initial climb, keep with the deer's head waymarks through an area of mature conifers to a cross-roads. Turn right, and rejoin the shorter walk.

Continue to the edge of the forest. Go left over a stile and descend through fields to arrive at Chalton opposite the **Red Lion**. Follow the Compton road eastwards, and, just before the top of the rise, go left on a field path that drops to a road. Cross the railway on a concrete bridge to Woodcroft Farm. Take the bridleway running forward along the valley bottom. Slip into trees: at the beginning of a woodland ride an SBP sign welcomes you. The ride finally winds to the left: at the iron gate, leave the bird signs and bear right on another bridleway that exits the trees. To the rear of Ladyholt, turn sharp left on a track to Eckensfield. Turn back left towards the trees, edge beside the wood and once inside, swing right. Go left at a junction, then, between the gates, keep ahead. The second path on the right drops down to the site of an old barn: enter a belt of trees for a long shady walk that reaches the outward route. Turn right to reverse the SDW back to the start.

POINTS OF INTEREST:

Country Park – The Queen Elizabeth Country Park covers 1400 acres and is managed by Hampshire County Council in partnership with Forest Enterprise (the Forestry Commission). Butser Hill, west of the A3, is connected by tunnel to the rest of the Park. At its foot is a reconstructed ancient farm where old forms of agriculture are practised and theories tested. The wooded War and Holt Downs are more geared to the enjoyment of a forest environment. Separate trails are provided for the walkers, riders and mountain bikers. The Park was named from woodlands planted in 1952 on War Down to mark the Coronation, although the first plantings on the hill had been made in 1928.

Red Lion – This thatched inn is reputed to be the oldest in Hampshire. It is thought to have been built as a workshop for the craftsmen who built the church.

REFRESHMENTS:

The Red Lion, Chalton.
The Country Park café.